SCOTS-FRENCH LINKS
in
EUROPE and AMERICA

1550 - 1850

ENGLAND

London

ENGLISH CHANNEL

FLANDERS

Calais

Boulogne

ARTOIS

NETHERLANDS

Brussels

R. MEUSE

R. RHINE

Amiens

Cateau-Cambrésis

THE

Arques

St. Quentin

Sedan

HOLY

LeHavre Rouen

PICARDY

Luxembourg

ROMAN

Honfleur

Soissons

Verdun

Metz

EMPIRE

Caen

Reims

NORMANDY

ILE-DE

St.Denis R. MARNE Châlons

Vassy

Nancy

Strasburg

Paris

FRANCE

Joinville

Toul

LORRAINE

ALSACE

St. Malo

Chartres

CHAMPAGNE

St. Aubin

MAINE

Troyes

FRANCHE

Rennes

Sablé

Dijon

BRITTANY

Orléans

Montargis

COMTÉ

Vannes

Auxerre

SWISS

R. LOIRE

Angers Tours

NIVERNAIS

BURGUNDY

CANTONS

Nantes

ANJOU

TOURAINE

Bourges

BERRY

Nevers

Saumur

Poitiers

Mâcon

Geneva

POITOU

Moulins

BRESSE

AUNIS

Lyon

DUCHY OF

La Rochelle

Limoges

SAVOY

Saintes

Jarnac

AUVERGNE

Clermont

DUCHY

Romans

OF

ANGOULEME

LIMOUSIN

R. LOIRE

Grenoble

SALUZZO

Périgueux

Valence

Coutras

SAINTONGE

PÉRIGORD

R. RHONE

Bordeaux

Le

DAUPHINÉ

GUYENNE

Puy

Nérac

Gap

GARONNE R.

Cahors

Avignon

Nice

BAY OF

Lodève

PROVENCE

BISCAY

Bayonne

GASCONY

Montpellier

Aix-en-Provence

Toulouse

LANGUEDOC

Marseille

BASSE-

Toulon

NAVARRE

Narbonne

HAUTE

MEDITERRANEAN

NAVARRE

Perpignan

SEA

SPAIN

ROUSSILLON

N

France in 1614

SCOTS-FRENCH LINKS

in

EUROPE and AMERICA

1550 - 1850

By
David Dobson

CLEARFIELD

Reprinted for Clearfield Company by
Genealogical Publishing Company
Baltimore, Maryland
2011

ISBN 978-0-8063-5528-3

Made in the United States of America

INTRODUCTION

Scotland has had strong economic and social links with France since the medieval period which led to settlement by Scots there.

During the medieval period many Scottish soldiers fought for France, for example during the Hundred Years War between England and France. Subsequently some of the survivors settled there, for example Nicholas Chambers was granted the seigneury of Guerche in Touraine in 1444. Other Scottish families that settled in France included Kinninmond [as Quinemont], Gowrie [Gohory], Dougla [Du Glas], Drummond [Drumont], Crawford [de Crafort], Lockhart [Locart], Turnbull [Torneboule] and Ramsay [de Ramezay]. During the early modern period France continued to attract Scottish soldiers, for example In August 1627, 2,000 Scottish soldiers under William, 6th Earl of Morton, were despatched to France to assist the Huguenots who were besieged in La Rochelle. In the eighteenth century many Jacobites fled to France, some of whom enrolled in French regiments.

Economic opportunities in France attracted Scottish merchants who generally settled in ports such as Rouen, Dunkirk, Bordeaux, Dieppe and Calais, while others were attracted to Paris. Scholars were attracted by the universities of France and after the Reformation in Scotland Catholic families often sent their sons to France to be educated at seminaries there, such as the Scots Colleges in Paris and in Douai. To a lesser extent Scotland attracted French immigrants, many of were Huguenot refugees. Scots could also be found in the French colonies in the Americas during the seventeenth and eighteenth centuries.

This book identifies some of the Scots who settled in France and its colonies in the Americas between 1550 and 1850. It also contains references to a number of Frenchmen found in contemporary Scotland.

David Dobson,
Dundee, Scotland, 2011

REFERENCES

Archives

ACA	=	Aberdeen City Archives
DUAS	=	Dundee University Archival Service
ECA	=	Edinburgh City Archives
NA	=	National Archives, London
NAS	=	National Archives of Scotland, Edinburgh
NLS	=	National Library of Scotland, Edinburgh
NSARM	=	Nova Scotia Archives & Records Management
STAUL	=	St Andrews University Library

Publications

ABR	=	Ayr Burgess Roll
AJ	=	Aberdeen Journal, series
ASS	=	Archieven van Sint Eustatius
BBC	=	Blairs of Balthyock and their Cadets, 1150-1850, Baltimore, 2001]
CM	=	Caledonian Mercury, series
CRA	=	Jacobite Cess Roll of Aberdeen, 1715
CRP	=	Cheap of Rossie Papers, ms
DCB	=	Dictionary of Canadian Biography
EA	=	Edinburgh Advertiser, series

EEC	=	Edinburgh Evening Courant, series
F	=	Fastii Ecclesiae Scoticanae
FH	=	Fife Herald, series
GK	=	Goteborg, Skottland och vackre Prinsen
GM	=	Gentleman's Magazine, series
IR	=	Innes Review, series
JAB	=	Jacobites of Aberdeen and Banff
JAHR	=	Journal of Army Historical Research
JP	=	Jacobite Peerage, Edinburgh, 1904
LPR	=	List of Prisoners of the Rebellion, 1890
MHP	=	Military History of Perthshire
MR	=	Muster Roll
MSC	=	Miscellany of the Spalding Club
NWI	=	New World Immigrants
OR	=	The Forfarshire or Lord Ogilvy's Regiment, Forfar, 1914
P	=	Prisoners of the '45, Edinburgh, 1928
PCC	=	Prerogative Court of Canterbury
RSC	=	Records of the Scots Colleges, Aberdeen, 1906
RGS	=	Register of the Great Seal of Scotland
RPCS	=	Register of the Privy Council of Scotland,
S	=	Scotsman, series

SA	=	Scotland and the Americas, 1650-1939, [Edinburgh, 2002]
SABR	=	St Andrews Burgess Roll
SCP	=	Scots College in Paris, 1603-1792
SE	=	Scotland and Europe, Scotland in Europe, [Cambridge, 2007]
SIL	=	Letterbook of bailie John Steuart of Inverness, 1715-1752, W. Mackay, [Edinburgh, 1915]
SM	=	Scots Magazine, series
TGSI	=	Transactions of the Gaelic Society of Inverness, series
W	=	Witness, series

SCOTS-FRENCH LINKS
IN EUROPE AND AMERICA
1550-1850

ABERCROMBIE, JOHN, a prisoner in Edinburgh Tolbooth who was released to go to France as a soldier on 4 February 1676. [RPCS.3/1V.668]

ABERCROMBY, PATRICK, born 1671, son of Alexander Abercromby of Fetternear, a student at the Scots College at Douai, 1685. [RSC.I.58]

ABERNETHY, ADAM, a student at Montpellier University, 1611. [RCPE]

ABERNETHY, JOHN, from Caithness, a student at Montpellier and Orange Universities, 1634. [RCPE]

ABERNETHY, ..., a Captain of *Le Regiment d'Ogilvie*, 1747. [JAHR]

ADAM, GEORGE, a soldier of the Grenadier Company of *Le Regiment d'Albanie*, 1748. [JAHR]

ADAM, ROBERT, born 1729, a Jacobite from Stirling in 1745, transported from Liverpool on the <u>Veteran</u> bound for the Leeward Islands on 5 May 1747, liberated and landed on Martinique in June 1747. [NA.SP.36.102]

ADAMSON, GEORGE, servant to James Browne, a factor at Bordeaux, a bond, 1669. [NAS.RD4.24.367]

ADINSTON, MARGARET, relict of Francis Kinloch a merchant in Paris, deeds, 1674,1697. [NAS.RD4.176/2.238; RD3.86.711]

AGNEW, ROBERT VANS, a merchant in Bordeaux around 1787.

AIKMAN, THOMAS, a cadet of the Douglas Regiment in French Service, 1671. [NAS.NRAS#0/174]

AINSLIE, GEORGE, a factor in Bordeaux, was admitted as a burgess of St Andrews on 5 July 1727, [SABR]; a merchant in Bordeaux, 1720s; 1731, 1742, 1764, 1765. [NAS.NRAS.2362/316; AC10.189; RS35.16.456; RD2.197.107, RD2.197.107; RD2.198.395]

AINSLIE, JAMES, from Edinburgh, a student at Orange University, 1639. [RCPE]

AINSLIE, ROBERT, from Edinburgh, a student at Montpellier University, 1631. [RCPE]

AINSLIE, ROBERT, a merchant in Bordeaux, 1731. [NAS.AC10.189]

AITCHISON, GEORGE, born 1797 in Dryfesdale, Dumfries-shire, son of John Aitchison in Borland, died in Guadaloupe during June 1816. [Dryfesdale MI]

ALBERT, JOHN, son of Daniel Albert, a merchant in Bordeaux, a deed, 1686. [NAS.RD4.57.711]

ALEXANDER, ANDREW, a factor and merchant in La Rochelle, 1674, 1682, then in Edinburgh, 1684. [NAS.RD3.53.151; AC7.6][UStA.CRP.I.7/62B]

ALEXANDER, JAMES, a merchant in Paris,1677, later in Edinburgh, 1686. [NAS.AC7.4; AC7.7]

ALEXANDER, JOHN, from Aberdeen, a student at Rheims University, 1681. [RCPE]

ALEXANDER, WILLIAM, graduated MD from Rheims University, 1706. [NAS.NRAS.726.3.18]

ALEXANDER, WILLIAM, attorney for Louis D'Hardanwart, director of the Maritime and Commercial Assurance Company of Paris, a deed, 1765. [NAS.RD4.197/1.909]

ALLAN, JAMES, a student at the Scots College at Douai, 1793. [IR.LVIII.223]

ALVES, WILLIAM, a student at Rheims University, 1749. [RCPE]

AMAVET, or COURTENAY, ANN, in Toulouse, a deed of factory, 1851. [NAS.SC57.40.200]

AMAVET, JOSEPH BONIFACE, professor of music in Toulouse, a deed of factory, 1851. [NAS.SC57.40.200]

ANDERSON, ALEXANDER, from Aberdeen, a student at Rheims University, 1620. [RCPE]

ANDERSON, JAMES, born 1722, a tailor from Ross-shire, a Jacobite in 1745, transported from Liverpool on the Veteran bound for the Leeward Islands on 5 May 1747, liberated and landed on Martinique in June 1747. [P.2.12][NA.SP.36.102]

ANDERSON, JAMES, a saddler in Paris, son of William Anderson a saddler in Haddington, East Lothian, 1830; dead by 1837. [NAS.SH.1830]

ANDERSON, JOHN, born 1729, a gardener, a Jacobite in 1745, transported from Liverpool on the Veteran bound for the Leeward Islands on 5 May 1747, liberated and landed on Martinique in June 1747. [P.2.12][NA.SP.36.102][JAB.2.419][MR.69]

ANDERSON, JOHN, born 2 October 1796 in Newburgh, Fife, a minister who died in Nice on 16 March 1834. [Newburgh MI]

ANDERSON, ROBERT, a weaver, son of Robert Anderson a weaver, burgess and guilds-brother, was admitted as a burgess of Glasgow on 27 September 1627 as he had gone as a soldier to aid in the relief of La Rochelle. [GBR]

ANDERSON, ROBERT, a saddler in Paris, son of William Anderson a saddler in Haddington, East Lothian, 1837. [NAS.SH.1837]

ANDREE, CHRISTOPHE, a French seaman aboard the Pylade, captured in Cayenne, French Guiana, a prisoner of war in Esk Mills, Scotland, died there 7 April 1811. [NA.ADM.103.124/1255, 103.548]

ANNAND, THOMAS, son of William Annand of Tolhill and his wife Janet King, a student in Paris, 1601. [MSC.ii.55]

ANNAND, THOMAS, from Edinburgh, a gentleman of the King of France's Guard, 1664, [NAS.RD4.11.122]; testament confirmed in Edinburgh on 28 June 1664. [NAS.CC8.8.-]

ARBUTHNOTT, ALEXANDER, son of Nathaniel Arbuthnott and his wife Elspet Duncan, a litster in Peterhead, Aberdeenshire, a Jacobite in 1715 who fled to France in 1716. [JAB#18]

ARBUTHNOT, ROBERT, a factor or merchant in Rouen, deeds, 1702, 1705, later in Paris, 1723, probably a Jacobite in the service of the Earl of Panmure. [NAS.RD2.86.397, RD3.107.305; E650.79; NRAS.332/C3/759] [HMC.Stuart Papers.II.440] [SIL#48]

ARBUTHNOTT, THOMAS, from Edinburgh, a student at Rheims University, 1739. [RCPE]

ARBUTHNOT, ..., an officer of *Le Regiment Royal Ecossais*, 1744. [JAHR]

ARCHIBALD, PATRICK, in Leith, formerly a factor in Bordeaux, a deed, 1693. [NAS.RD4.82.957]

ARMOUR, JEREMY, from Edinburgh, a student at Rheims University, 1736. [RCPE]

ARNOULT, STEPHAN, a factor in Rouen, was admitted as a burgess and guilds-brother of Ayr on 7 June 1686. [ABR]

ARNOUS, PIERRE, a French teacher who settled in
Edinburgh 1779, residing in Baillie Fife's Close in 1794.
[ECA.SL115.1.1]

ARTHUR, Sir DANIEL, a banker in Paris, a deed, 1700.
[NAS.RD4.86.368]

ATKINSON, JOHN, a student at Rheims University, 1732.
[RCPE]

AUSTINDIN, DAVID, a Captain of the Scots Guards of
France, 1560s. [NAS.NRAS.0.143]

AYMAR, PETER AUGUSTUS, born 1775, Captain and
Adjutant Major of the French Army, a prisoner of war on
parole in Lanark, died 23 September 1813. [Lanark MI]

BADENOCH, ALEXANDER, a student at the Scots College
at Douai in 1793, later rector of the college at
Aquhorties. [IR.LVIII.223]

BAILLIE, ..., an officer of *Le Regiment Royal Ecossais*,
1744. [JAHR]

BACHOP, DUNCAN, a student at Rheims University, 1725.
[RCPE]

BAGNELL, EDWARD, a merchant, formerly in St Pierre,
Martinique, then in Trinidad, a deed, 1817.
[NAS.RD5.115.444]

BAILLIE, ROBERT, a student at Rheims University, 1713.
[RCPE]

BAIN, GEORGE, born 21 June 1722 son of Alexander Bain in
Kemnay, Aberdeenshire, a laborer and a Jacobite in
1745, transported from Liverpool on the <u>Veteran</u> bound
for the Leeward Islands on 5 May 1747, liberated and
landed on Martinique in June 1747.
[P.2.220][NA.SP.36.102][JAB.2.419]

BAIRD, HENRY, a merchant in Paris, a deed, 1700.
[NAS.RD2.84.253]

BAIRD, JAMES, graduated MD from Rheims University, 1737. [NAS.NRAS.726.3.61]

BAIRD, Captain WILLIAM, son of Sir James Baird of Saughtonhall, died in Boulogne-sur-Mer on 20 May 1813. [SM.86.776]

BALFOUR, ANDREW, from Fife, a student at Caen University, 1661. [RCPE]

BALFOUR, ROBERT, born near Dundee in 1550, educated at the universities of St Andrews and of Paris, an academic at the College of Guienne, Bordeaux, died after 1625. [NAS.NA21951]

BALFOUR, ROBERT, a student at Rheims University, 1718. [RCPE]

BALFOUR, ..., daughter of James Craig Balfour, was born in Villa de Calvaire, St Servan, France, on 31 January 1898. [S#17039]

BANNERMAN, JOHN, from Inverness, a student at Rheims University, 1707. [RCPE]

BARCLAY, CHARLES, born 30 July 1790, son of Reverend Peter Barclay and his wife Margaret Duddingston in Kettle, Fife, died at Pointe au Petre, Guadaloupe, on 13 June 1819. [F.5.160][EEC#16877][S.3.134]

BARCLAY, WILLIAM, from Aberdeen, a student at Caen University, 1609. [RCPE]

BEAN, JOHN, born in Balquimey, a Sergeant of *Le Regiment d'Ogilvie*, 1747. [JAHR]

BEATON, JAMES, an archer of the Scots Guards of France, 1560s. [NAS.NRAS.0.143]

BEATON, NEAL, a student at the Scots College in Paris from 1702 to 1704. [SCP.213]

BEATSON, DAVID, a Lieutenant of the Earl of
Dunfermline's Regiment in France, 1676; a Lieutenant
of the Scots Regiment in France, a bond, 1683.
[NAS.RD4.39.796; RD2.60.526]

BEAUCHESNE, THOMAS, an embroiderer in Canongate,
Edinburgh, husband of Helen Le Comte, 1688.
[NAS.RD3.69.112]

BECK, PHILIP, aged 21, born in Inverness, Scotland, a
Sergeant of *Le Regiment d'Ogilvie*, 17... [JAHR]

BELL, ADAM, a Lieutenant of the Earl of Dunfermline's
Regiment in France, 1676. [NAS.RD4.39.796]
BELL, BRYCE, a student at Caen University, 1669. [RCPE]

BELL, WILLIAM, born 1701, a bookseller in Berwickshire, a
Jacobite in 1745, transported from Liverpool on the
Veteran bound for the Leeward Islands on 5 May 1747,
liberated and landed on Martinique in June 1747.
[P.2.32][NA.SP.36.102]

BETH, JOHN, a soldier of the Grenadier Company of *Le
Regiment d'Albanie*, 1748. [JAHR]

BETHUNE, GEORGE, from Cupar, Fife, a student at Rheims
University, 1731. [RCPE]

BINGHAM, WILLIAM, in St Pierre, Martinique, 1779.
[NAS.NRAS.771/544]

BLACK, JOHN, a wine-merchant in Bordeaux, 1720s,
[NAS.NRAS.2362/316]; 1731; was admitted as a
burgess and guilds-brother of Ayr on 18 August 1752.
[NAS.AC9/1163][ABR]

BLACKBURN, DAVID, in Rouen, 1641. [NAS.GD18.2403]

BLACKWOOD, HENRY, a student at Paris University, 1568.
[RCPE]

BLAIR, Mr ALEXANDER, born ca1563 at Balthayock,
Perthshire, son of Alexander Blair of Balthayock and

Janet Ogilvie, graduated St Andrews 1578, settled in
France as Provost of the University of Lescar, died
ca1620. [BBC#100]

BLAIR, ALEXANDER, of Balmyle, a writer in Edinburgh,
then a merchant in Dunkirk, 1736. [NAS.RS35.15.574]

BLAIR, JAMES, a student at Rheims University, 1734.
[RCPE]

BLAIR, Dr ROBERT, physician to Lord Panmure, a Jacobite
who fought at Sheriffmuir in 1715, fled via Arbroath to
France. [JAB.24]

BLAIR, THOMAS, of Glassclune, Dundee, a Jacobite
Lieutenant Colonel in 1745, fled to Norway, imprisoned
in Bergen, later settled in France as a Captain of *Le
Regiment d'Ogilvie*, 1747. [JAHR][LPR#198][OR#127]

BLAIR, THOMAS, a merchant in Dunkirk, dead by 1768.
[NAS.GD80.656]

BLANZIE, PETER, a merchant in Bordeaux, a bond, 1672.
[NAS.RD2.33.112]

BOG, JOHN, an archer of the Scots Guards of France, 1560s.
[NAS.NRAS.0.143]

BOOTH, JAMES, in Martinique, later in Aberdeen, testament,
27 January 1812, Commissariat of Aberdeen. [NAS]

BOOTH, WILLIAM, a Captain of *Le Regiment Royal
Ecossais*, 1745-1747. [JAHR]

BORDENAVE, PIERRE, in Osses, Basses Pyrenees, France,
an inventory, 1872. [NAS.SC70.156/481]

BORDENAVE, PIERRE FINLAY, in Osses, Basses
Pyrenees, France, an inventory, 1874.
[NAS.SC70.169/602]

BOUCHEL, ANTHONY, a merchant in La Rochelle, a deed,
1682. [NAS.RD2.57.544]

BOWER, ALEXANDER, son of James Bower of Meathie, Angus, in France, 1730. [NAS.NRAS.16/2]

BOWER, ROBERT, from Kincaldrum, Angus, a student at Douai, 1772. [NAS.GD503.143]

BOWIE, JOHN, born 1733, a Jacobite in Aberdeen in 1745, transported from Liverpool on the Veteran bound for the Leeward Islands on 5 May 1747, liberated and landed on Martinique in June 1747. [P.2.44][NA.SP.36.102][JAB.2.420]

BOWIE, ROBERT, a merchant in Bordeaux, 1785. [NAS.RS17.123]

BOYACK, ROBERT, a surgeon in Brussels, 1768. [NAS.RS35.22/434]

BOYD, JOHN, sent by the King of France on the La Marie, Captain Tapic, to Louisiana on 28 May 1719, died on the voyage. [NWI.I.490]

BOYER, AUGUST, born 1821, an engineer, eldest son of Peter Boyer, an engineer in Lille, died there on 23 March 1863. [DPCA#4208]

BRARD, AUGUSTUS FRANCIS, born 1789 in Paris, died, probably, in Lanark on 26 August 1873, husband of Jean Currie, born 1790, died 29 September 1844. [Lanark gravestone]

BREHIEU, JEAN, born 1764 in Normandy to Edinburgh in 1794 to study physics, '5 feet 11 inches, thin made, swarthy smooth complexion, a mole on his left cheek, dark brown hair '.[ECA.SL115.1.1]

BROWN, ALEXANDER, a student at Rheims University, 1687. [RCPE]

BROWN, ANDREW, a merchant burgess of Perth, bound for France in 1633. [StAUL.MS36220/679; HL#679]

BROWN, GABRIEL ARMAUNDE, in Sens, France, heir to his grandfather William Brown of Nunton, 1756. [NAS.S/H]

BROWN, JAMES, a merchant in Bordeaux, 1630s-1640s; 1661. [NAS.GD18.2407/2371; RD2.1.726; RGS.X.11/20; SE#28]

BROWN, JAMES, a student at Rheims University, 1704. [RCPE]; graduated MD from Rheims University in 1706. [NAS.NRAS.726.3.16]

BROWN, JOSEPH, born 1731, a tailor from Banff, a Jacobite in 1745, transported from Liverpool on the Veteran bound for the Leeward Islands on 5 May 1747, liberated and landed on Martinique in June 1747. [P.2.54][NA.SP.36.102][JAB.2.420]

BROWN, ROBERT, a merchant in Bordeaux, 1630s-1640s. [NAS.GD18/2361; SE#28]

BROWN, WILLIAM, a Scottish merchant, trading with Bordeaux, 1593. [NAS.JC66.6]

BROWN, ..., a Captain of *Le Regiment d'Ogilvie*, 1747. [JAHR]

BROWNHILLS, THOMAS, born 1725, a laborer in Kinnaird, Inchture, Perthshire, a Jacobite in 1745, transported from Liverpool on the Veteran bound for the Leeward Islands on 5 May 1747, liberated and landed on Martinique in June 1747. [P.2.52][NA.SP.36.102]

BROWNLEE, ALEXANDER, son of Archibald Brownlee, a watchmaker in Edinburgh, a Jacobite in 1745, transported from Liverpool on the Veteran bound for the Leeward Islands on 5 May 1747, liberated and landed on Martinique in June 1747. [P.2.54][NA.SP.36.102][MR102]

BRUCE, GEORGE, from Anstruther, Fife, a student at Rheims University, 1702. [RCPE]

BRUCE, JAMES, in Martinique, probate 1797 PCC

BRUCE, ROBERT, a Lieutenant of a Scottish regiment in
France, 1671. [NAS.RD2.31.406]

BUCHAN, THOMAS, a Captain of a Scottish Regiment in
France, a deed of factory and a bond, 1675.
[NAS.RD2.40.373/429]

BUCHANAN, GEORGE, a student at Rheims University,
1733. [RCPE]

BUCHANAN, GEORGE, in Dunkirk, 1764.
[NAS.GD1.512.11]

BUCHANAN, Miss JANE, in St Germain-en-Laye, France,
died 20 February 1835, inventory, 1835, Comm.
Edinburgh. [NAS]

BUCHANAN of MENTEITH, ..., a Captain of *Le
Regiment d'Ogilvie*, 1747. [JAHR]

BUERT and LE BRUN, a deed, 1701. [NAS.RD4.89.711]

BURNETT, ALEXANDER, from Rayne, a student at the
Scots College at Douai, 1699. [RSC.I.199]

BURNET, THOMAS, a student at Montpellier University,
1659. [RCPE]

BURNEY, WILLIAM, aged 48, and his wife aged 46, with his
son William aged 28, his wife aged 25, and their children
John aged 8, Jack aged 6, and William aged 1, settled in
Louisiana in 1797. [NWI.II.231]

BURSE, FRANCOIS, a factor in France for John Slowan a
merchant in Edinburgh, 1628. [NAS.AC7.1.154]

BUTTI, PETER LOUIS, a student in Douai, France, heir to
his mother Elizabeth Mitchell who died on 9 May 1867,
wife of Louis Joseph Butti in Edinburgh, 1868.
[NAS.S/H]

CALDERWOOD, OLIVER, son of John Calderwood a bailie of Musselburgh, a student who died in Paris. [probate 1680 PCC]

CALINS, ALEXANDER, a student at Montpellier University, 1611. [RCPE]

CAMERON, ALEXANDER, born 1728, a cartwright in Drumnaglass, Inverness-shire, a Jacobite in 1745, transported from Liverpool on the Veteran bound for the Leeward Islands on 5 May 1747, liberated and landed on Martinique in June 1747. [P.2.70][NA.SP.36.102][MR174]

CAMERON, ALEXANDER, born in Callary, Inverness-shire, son of Allan Cameron and his wife Isabel Cameron, a Sergeant of the Grenadier Company of Le Regiment d'Albanie, 1748. [JAHR]

CAMERON, ALEXANDER, a Lieutenant of Grenadiers in Le Regiment d'Ogilvie, 1756. [JAHR]

CAMERON, ALLAN, a Lieutenant of Le Regiment Royal Ecossais, 1749-1760. [JAHR]

CAMERON, ANNE, born 1729, a spinner in Lochaber, Inverness-shire, a Jacobite in 1745, transported from Liverpool on the Veteran bound for the Leeward Islands on 5 May 1747, liberated and landed on Martinique in June 1747. [P.2.72][NA.SP.36.102]

CAMERON, ARCHIBALD, a Captain of Le Regiment d'Ogilvie, 1747. [JAHR]

CAMERON, CHARLES, a student at the Scots College at Douai, 1751. [RSC.I.88]

CAMERON, CHARLES, a Lieutenant of Grenadiers in Le Regiment d'Ogilvy, 1756. [JAHR]

CAMERON, DONALD, of Lochiel, a Jacobite in 1745, fled to France in 1746, Colonel of the Albany Regiment in

France, husband of Anne Campbell, died on 25 October 1748. [TGSI.XXI.133]

CAMERON, DONALD, a soldier of the Grenadier Company of *Le Regiment d'Albanie*, 1748. [JAHR]

CAMERON, DONALD, of Lochiel, died in Toulouse on 14 September 1832, inventory 1834, Comm. Edinburgh. [AJ#4426][FH#557]

CAMERON, EDWARD, from Duncross, Perthshire, a soldier in the Grenadier Company of *Le Regiment d'Albanie*, 1748. [JAHR]

CAMERON, EFFIE, born 1719, a spinner in Lochaber, Inverness-shire, a Jacobite in 1745, transported from Liverpool on the Veteran bound for the Leeward Islands on 5 May 1747, liberated and landed on Martinique in June 1747. [P.2.80][NA.SP.36.102]

CAMERON, FLORA, born 1707, a spinner in Lochaber, Inverness-shire, a Jacobite in 1745, transported from Liverpool on the Veteran bound for the Leeward Islands on 5 May 1747, liberated and landed on Martinique in June 1747. [P.2.80][NA.SP.36.102]

CAMERON, JAMES, son of Donald Cameron of Lochiel, a Captain of the Royal Regiment of Scots in France in 1744, died in 1759. [TGSI.XXI.133][JAHR]

CAMERON, JOHN, son of Sir Ewan Cameron of Lochiel and his wife Isabel MacLean, a Jacobite in 1715 who escaped to France, died in Flanders during 1748. [JP#77]

CAMERON, JOHN, of LOCHIEL, son of Donald Cameron of Lochiel, a Captain of the Albany Regiment of France, later in 1744 of the Royal Regiment of Scots in France, returned to Scotland in 1759, and died in 1762. [TGSI.XXI.133][JAHR]

CAMERON, JOHN ALEXANDER, a Captain of *Le Regiment d'Albanie*, 1748. [JAHR]

CAMERON, ..., a Lieutenant of Grenadiers in *Le Regiment d'Ogilvy*, 1747. [JAHR]

CAMPBELL, ADAM, a student at Montpellier and Orange Universities, 1610s. [RCPE]

CAMPBELL, ALEXANDER, a student at Rheims University, 1736. [RCPE]

CAMPBELL, ALEXANDER, born 1707, a weaver in Argyll, a Jacobite in 1745, transported from Liverpool on the Veteran bound for the Leeward Islands on 5 May 1747, liberated and landed on Martinique in June 1747. [P.2.88][NA.SP.36.102]

CAMPBELL, ALEXANDER, born 1720, a labourer in Argyll, a Jacobite in 1745, transported from Liverpool on the Veteran bound for the Leeward Islands on 5 May 1747, liberated and landed on Martinique in June 1747. [NA.SP.36.102]

CAMPBELL, ANNE, youngest daughter of George James Campbell of Treesbanks, Ayrshire, died in Paris on 14 January 1845. [W#546]

CAMPBELL, Captain ARCHIBALD MONTGOMERY, in Dieppe, died 7 Aug.1832, inventory, 1832, Comm. Edinburgh. [NAS]

CAMPBELL, ARTHUR MAXWELL, son of Colonel Campbell of Avizyards, Ayrshire, died in Valence on the Rhone on 9 July 1841. [EEC#20242]

CAMPBELL, BARBARA, born 1728, a spinner in Perthshire, a Jacobite in 1745, transported from Liverpool on the Veteran bound for the Leeward Islands on 5 May 1747, liberated and landed on Martinique in June 1747. [P.2.90][NA.SP.36.102]

CAMPBELL, BARBARA, Countess Jules de Polignac, youngest daughter of Duncan Campbell in Edinburgh, and only sister of Mrs Archibald Macdonald in London. She married Count Jules de Polignac, second son to the late Duke de Polignac, in London, and died 23 May 1819 at St Maude, near Paris, aged 21. [SM.NS.IV.587]

CAMPBELL, COLIN, of Lochnell, born 1689, a student at the Scots College in Paris, 1716, ordained as a priest in Paris during 1722, a priest in the Highlands, killed at the Battle of Culloden in 1746. [SCP.214][NAS.NRAS.771.bundle#814]

CAMPBELL, COLIN, son of Robert Campbell (1726-1782) and his wife Jean Sinclair, a surgeon of the 39th Regiment, who died in Guadaloupe in 1794. [SP.II.199]

CAMPBELL, DOUGALD, MD, youngest son of John Campbell of Glendaddle and Newfield, died in Boulogne-sur-Mer on 22 May 1847. [EEC#21510]

CAMPBELL, DOUGALL, born 1729, a servant in Lochaber, Inverness-shire, a Jacobite in 1745, transported from Liverpool on the Veteran bound for the Leeward Islands on 5 May 1747, liberated and landed on Martinique in June 1747. [P.2.90][NA.SP.36.102]

CAMPBELL, DUNCAN, born 1731, a laborer in Argyll, a Jacobite in 1745, transported from Liverpool on the Veteran bound for the Leeward Islands on 5 May 1747, liberated and landed on Martinique in June 1747. [P.2.92][NA.SP.36.102]

CAMPBELL, FRANCIS GARDEN, of Troup and Glenlyon, died at Tivoli Retine, Bordeaux, on 28 May 1815. [SM.77.559]

CAMPBELL, GEORGE, a merchant in Brussels, a deed, 1694. [NAS.RD4.74.508]

CAMPBELL, JAMES, in Rouen, 1642. [NAS.GD18.2416]

CAMPBELL, JAMES, a Captain of the Earl of Dunfermline's Regiment of Scots in France, 1676. [NAS.RD4.39.200]

CAMPBELL, JOHN, from Edinburgh, a student at Rheims University, 1742. [RCPE]

CAMPBELL, JOHN, born 1727, a laborer in Inverness, a Jacobite in 1745, transported from Liverpool on the Veteran bound for the Leeward Islands on 5 May 1747, liberated and landed on Martinique in June 1747. [P.2.94][NA.SP.36.102]

CAMPBELL, JOHN, born 1732, a servant in Rannoch, Argyll, a Jacobite in 1745, transported from Liverpool on the Veteran bound for the Leeward Islands on 5 May 1747, liberated and landed on Martinique in June 1747. [P.2.96][NA.SP.36.102][MR151]

CAMPBELL, JOHN, of Blythswood, Lieutenant Colonel of the 6th Regiment of Foot, died at the taking of Martinique, 1794. [SM.56.236]

CAMPBELL, MARTHA, born 1858, daughter of Matthew Campbell and his wife Flora Eglinton, died in Pau on 8 December 1874. [Gourock MI]

CAMPBELL, Captain NEAL H.P., 78th Regiment of Foot, died in France, 18 September 1834, inventory, 1834, Comm. Edinburgh. [NAS]

CAMPBELL, PATRICK, a student at Rheims University, 1728. [RCPE]

CAMPBELL, ROBERT, a student at Rheims University, 1720. [RCPE]

CAMPBELL, THOMAS, LL.D., in Boulogne-sur-Mer, died 15 June 1844, inventory, 1845, Comm. Edinburgh. [NAS]

CAMPBELL, WILLIAM, born 1726, a weaver in Grantully, Perthshire, a Jacobite in 1745, transported from Liverpool on the Veteran bound for the Leeward Islands on 5 May 1747, liberated and landed on Martinique in June 1747. [P.2.98][NA.SP.36.102][MR206]

CAMPBELL, ..., a Captain of Grenadiers in *Le Regiment d'Ogilvie*, 1747. [JAHR]

CAMPBELL, ..., surgeon of the Royal Artillery, died in St Domingo, 1796. [NAS.GD188.28.6]

CARMICHAEL, JAMES, a student at Rheims University, 1731. [RCPE]

CARMICHAEL, JAMES, in Ailly-sur-Somme, an inventory, 1876. [NAS.SC70.180/508]

CARMICHAEL, THOMAS, a student at Rheims University, 1725. [RCPE]

CARNEGIE, CHARLES, a Lieutenant of Panmure's Regiment of Foot in 1715, a Jacobite who settled in Lille in 1716. [NAS.GD45.1.201]

CARNEGIE, DAVID, a Captain of *Le Regiment d'Ogilvie,* 1747. [JAHR]

CARNEGIE, JAMES, Earl of Southesk, born on 4 April 1692, son of Charles Carnegie and his wife Mary Maitland, a Jacobite who fought at Sheriffmuir in 1715, fled to France in 1716. [JAB#189]

CARNEGY, JAMES, born 1668, son of William Carnegy a writer in Edinburgh, a student at the Scots College at Douai, 1688, died 1730s. [RSC.I.60]

CARRINE, FRANCIS, born in Dole, valet to Captain Cameron of Lochiel of the Duke of Gordon's Fencibles stationed at Edinburgh Castle in 1794. [ECA.SL115.1.1]

CARRON, JAMES, late a skipper in Leith, converted to Catholicism in 1694, 'went to France about two and a half years ago and never returned since', 1704. [NAS.CH1.2.5.2.149]

CARRUTHERS, THOMAS, a student at Rheims University, 1730. [RCPE]

CARSTAIRS, ..., Ensign of the Royal Scots Guards of France, 1663. [NAS.GD29.42]

CARSWELL, SAMUEL, aged 35, his wife aged 34, and their children Jean aged 10, Robert aged 5, and Matthew aged 3, settled in Louisiana in 1797. [NWI.II.228]

CATTENACH, ALEXANDER, born 1730, a miller in Badenoch, Inverness-shire, a Jacobite in 1745, transported from Liverpool on the Veteran bound for the Leeward Islands on 5 May 1747, liberated and landed on Martinique in June 1747. [P.2.104][NA.SP.36.102]

CAUVIN, LEWIS, second son of the late Lewis Cauvin a teacher of French in Edinburgh, a decreet, 1782. [NAS.CS17.1.1/76]

CHALMERS, ALEXANDER, from Edinburgh, graduated MA from Edinburgh University in 1676, a medical student at Rheims University, 1681, testament confirmed with the Commissariat of Edinburgh in 1714.[NAS] [RCPE]

CHALMERS, ISABEL, born 1722, a knitter in Mearns, a Jacobite in 1745, transported from Liverpool on the Veteran bound for the Leeward Islands on 5 May 1747, liberated and landed on Martinique in June 1747. [P.2.108][NA.SP.36.102]

CHALMERS, JOHN, born 1726, a labourer in Perthshire, a Jacobite in 1745, transported from Liverpool on the Veteran bound for the Leeward Islands on 5 May 1747, liberated and landed on Martinique in June 1747. [P.2.110][NA.SP.36.102]

CHALMERS, ..., a Lieutenant of *Le Regiment Royal Ecossais*, 1760. [JAHR]

CHAPLAIN, WILLIAM, a student at Rheims University, 1733. [RCPE]

CHARTERS, ALEXANDER, a merchant in Paris, a bond, 1670. [NAS.RD4/warrant #1612]

CHARTERIS, L., possibly from Edinburgh, a prisoner in the Castle of Brest, 1706. [NAS.RH1/2.763]

CHIFFELLE, FRANCOIS LOUIS, died 26 September 1838, husband of Elizabeth Whyte [1808-1859], father of Hannah Elizabeth Chiffelle. [Kirkcaldy Abbotshall MI]

CLAPERTON, WILLIAM, born 1734, a ploughboy from Fochabers, Banffshire, a Jacobite in 1745, transported from Liverpool on the Veteran bound for the Leeward Islands on 5 May 1747, liberated and landed on Martinique in June 1747. [P.2.116][NA.SP.36.102][MR122][JAB.2.135]

CLARK, JAMES, in Bordeaux, father of Margaret Clark in Libberton parish, 1676. [NAS.RD2.41.584]

CLARK, WILLIAM, from Glasgow, a student at Rheims University, 1736. [RCPE]

CLAVERING, ELIZABETH, born 1725, a seamstress in Banff, a Jacobite in 1745, transported from Liverpool on the Veteran bound for the Leeward Islands on 5 May 1747, liberated and landed on Martinique in June 1747. [P.2.118][NA.SP.36.102][JAB.2.422]

CLEGHORN, ..., a physician, died in St Domingo, 1796. [NAS.GD188.28.6]

CLELAND, or HENDERSON, Mrs M., in Brussels, an inventory, 1876. [NAS.SC70.181/21]

CLELAND, WILLIAM, son of Robert Cleland of Pedenie and his wife Jane Henderson, settled in Martinique by 1729. [NAS.GD172.978]

CLERK, JOHN, a merchant in Paris, 1634-1639, trading with Rouen, Dieppe, Bordeaux, Edinburgh and London. [NAS.GD18/2361; SE#29]

CLERK, WILLIAM, born 1668, son of William Clerk and Joanna Cars in Edinburgh, a student at the Scots College at Douai, 1688. [RSC.I.60]

CLERY, JEAN ANTHONY, a mariner on the Happy Amede of Martego, 1701, 1714. [NAS.RD4.89.348; RD4.89.348]

COATS, WILLIAM, born 1692, a laborer in Aberdeenshire, a Jacobite in 1745, transported from Liverpool on the Veteran bound for the Leeward Islands on 5 May 1747, liberated and landed on Martinique in June 1747. [P.2.120][NA.SP.36.102][JAB.2.422]

COCHRANE, CHARLES, a student at Rheims University, 1725. [RCPE]

COCHRANE, PETER, of Cleppings, died in France, 18 June 1831, inventory, 1834, Comm. Edinburgh. [NAS]

COCHRANE, WILLIAM, a student at Rheims University, 1712; graduated MD in 1714. [RCPE][NAS.NRAS.726.3.30]

COCKBURN, JOHN, in Dieppe, 1642. [NAS.GD18.2417]

COCKBURN, PATRICK, a law student in Paris, deeds, 1688, 1690. [NAS.RD3.67.516; RD2.71.1155]

COLLISON, GEORGE, born 1678, son of Robert Collison and Margaret Duguid in Aberdeen, a student at the Scots College at Douai, 1693. [RSC.I.62]

COLQUHOUN, JOHN, from Glasgow, a student at Orange University, 1654. [RCPE]

COLQUHOUN, WILHELMINA, wife of John Campbell of Stonefield, died in Pau, France, 22 December1833, inventory, 1834, Comm. Edinburgh, [NAS]

COLVILLE, GEORGE, a student at Rheims University, 1733. [RCPE]

COLVILLE, Captain JAMES, "ane pretendit office of conservatore at the toun of Caleis", in 1602. [SU#28]

COMRIE, ARCHIBALD, a student at Rheims University, 1713. [RCPE]

COMRIE, WILLIAM, a student at Rheims University, 1693. [RCPE]

COOK, JOHN, in Rouen, 1714. [NAS.RD4.89.377]

COPLAND, CHARLES, from Aberdeen, a cooper in Ostend, 1790. [NAS.S/H]

CORSSLE, RAFEAUX, a mariner on the Happy Amede of Martego, 1701. [NAS.RD4.89.348]

COUGRE, BALTIZAR, a mariner on the Happy Amede of Martego, 1701, 1714. [NAS.RD4.89.348]

COULT, OLIVER, MD, in Bantargu-sur-Mer in 1764. [NAS.RS27.165.43]

COUPER, JAMES, a merchant in Paris, a bond, 1672. [NAS.RD2.32.541]

COUTTS, WILLIAM, a student at the Scots College at Douai, 1742. [RSC.I.85]

COWPER, JAMES, from Edinburgh, a student at Rheims University, 1731. [RCPE]

CRAIG, ..., hospital mate, in St Domingo, 1796. [NAS.GD188.28.6]

CRAIGIE, WILLIAM, from Edinburgh, a student at Rheims University, 1738. [RCPE]

CRAUFORD, DAVID, from Ayr, a student at Rheims University, 1726. [RCPE]

CRAUFORD, DAVID, from Symington, Lanarkshire, a student at Rheims University, 1696. [RCPE]

CRAWFORD, DAVID, from Edinburgh, a student at Rheims University, 1717. [RCPE]

CRAWFORD, or DUNCAN, MARY S., in France, will, 8 February 1886. [NAS.SC70/6]

CRAWFORD, THOMAS, from Edinburgh, a student at Rheims University, 1712; graduated MD in 1714. [RCPE][NAS.NRAS.726.3.14]

CRICHTON, or JACKSON, MATILDA, in Dunkirk, daughter of Helen Scott or Jackson in Dundee who died on 7 November 1880. [NAS.S/H]

CROOKSHANK, ALEXANDER, rector of the Scots College at Douai, 1748. [RSC.I.86]

CRUDEN, GEORGE, in Martinique, 1799. [SA#260]

CRUICKSHANK, JOHN, from Huntly, a student at Rheims University, 1725. [RCPE]

CRUICKSHANK, JOHN, born 1733, a herdsman in Aberdeen, a Jacobite in 1745, transported from Liverpool on the Veteran bound for the Leeward Islands on 5 May 1747, liberated and landed on Martinique in June 1747. [P.2.138][NA.SP.36.102]

CUMMING, WILLIAM, a Captain of *Le Regiment Royal Ecossais*, 1745-1761. [JAHR]

CUMMING, Lieutenant, married Baroness Judith De Bretton, eldest daughter of Baron Frederick de Bretton in St Croix, in Guadaloupe in 1812. [GM.81.188]

CUNNINGHAM, ADAM, Captain in the service of the King of France, formerly in Carsgoe, 13 December 1677. [NAS.RS20.1.40]

CUNNINGHAM, CHARLES, in Cangee, France, was admitted as a burgess and guilds-brother of Ayr on 25 October 1658. [ABR]

CUNNINGHAM, JOHN, born 1715, from Argyll, a Jacobite in 1745, transported from Liverpool on the Veteran bound for the Leeward Islands on 5 May 1747, liberated

and landed on Martinique in June 1747.
[P.2.140][NA.SP.36.102][MR70]

CUNNINGHAM, ROBERT, of the Scots Guards in France,
1560s. [NAS.NRAS.0.143]

CUNNINGHAM, W. FAIRLIE, the younger of Robertland,
Ayrshire, died in Boulogne-sur-Mere on 1 October 1841.
[AJ#4898]

CUNNINGHAM, WILLIAM, born in France during 1838, a
medical student in Edinburgh, 1851. [Census]

CURRIE, ARCHIBALD, from Argyll, a merchant in New
York, died in Martinique in 1802. [EA#4048]

CUTHBERT of CASTLEHILL, ..., Lieutenant Colonel of
Le Regiment Royal Ecossais, 1747. [JAHR]

DALBRET, THOMAS, from Edinburgh, a student at Orange
University, 1634. [RCPE]

DALMAHOY, ..., a Captain of *Le Regiment Royal Ecossais,*
1745-1747. [JAHR]

DALRYMPLE, Colonel CAMPBELL, former Governor of
Guadaloupe, 1764. [NAS.RS27.166.335; RGS.107.119]

DALRYMPLE, THOMAS, a student at Caen University,
1688. [RCPE]

D'ASSAUVILLE, DUNCAN, a soldier of the 70th Regiment
of Foot, eldest son and heir of the deceased Nicholas
D'Assauville a weaver in Picardy, Edinburgh, and his
brothers James, Nicholas, and William D'Assauville,
1793. [NAS.NG1.66.5]

DAVIDSON, ALEXANDER, born 1730, a herdsman in
Badenoch, Inverness-shire, a Jacobite in 1745,
transported from Liverpool on the <u>Veteran</u> bound for the
Leeward Islands on 5 May 1747, liberated and landed on
Martinique in June 1747. [P.2.144][NA.SP.36.102]

DAVIDSON, CHARLES, first master of the Household of the Prince of Conde, a deed, 1700. [NAS.RD2.84.517]

DAVIDSON, JESSIE, wife of Robert Kevan in Ibroxholm, Glasgow, died in Tours on 9 January 1851. [W#1183]

DAVISON, ALEXANDER, a student at Rheims University, 1680. [RCPE]

DAVISON, ..., Lieutenant of the 1st [Royal Scots] Regiment, died in St Domingo, 1796. [NAS.GD188.28.6]

DE BAUSSET, LOUIS, born in Nantes, France, a Lieutenant captured on Martinique, a prisoner of war in Edinburgh Castle, escaped but recaptured in 1811, sent to Chatham. [NA.ADM.103.112/8; 103.124/2061]

DE CANTON, JAMES, a French master in Edinburgh, a deed, 1697. [NAS.RD4.81.140]

DE COCKBURN, GUILLAUME, born in St Domingo, French West Indies, in 1762, an officer of the French Navy, formerly a resident of Rochefort or Paris, moved to England in 1782, settled in Edinburgh by 1798. [ECA.SL115.2.1/2]

DE CORNET, JOHN, a broker in Bordeaux, was admitted as a burgess of Glasgow on 26 July 1630. [GBR]

DE COUDIS, ANTHONY, a mariner on the Happy Amede of Martego, 1701. [NAS.RD4.89.348]

D'EGVILLE, GUILLAUME, a teacher of dancing in Edinburgh, died 28 September 1853, inventories, 1853-1854, Comm. Edinburgh. [NAS]

DE FLANDRE, JEAN BAPTISTE, born 1811 in France, a French teacher in Edinburgh by 1851, his wife Maria C. de Flandre, born 1799 in France. [Census]

D'HEARCOURT, LOUIS CLAUDE D'ACHERY, a merchant in St Quentin, bailliage of Vermandois, France, testament, 12 February 1755, Comm. Edinburgh. [NAS]

DE LA COURT, ABRAHAM, was admitted as a burgess and guilds-brother of Ayr on 13 September 1662. [ABR]

DE LA FONTAINE, JACOB, a deed, 1697. [NAS.RD4.81.828]

DE LA PORTE, ATTALIE, born 1801 in Billom, Pays de Dome, France, a lady's maid in Edinburgh by 1851. [Census]

DE LA TOCNAYE, M., a former French Army officer, in Clackmannanshire 1794. [ECA.SL115.1.1]

DE LA TORRE, Don JOSE YGNACIA, in Bordeaux, died 16 February 1853, inventory, 1854, Comm. Edinburgh. [NAS]

DE LA TOUR, JEANNE, born 1801 in Billom de Dome, France, a silk cleaner in Edinburgh by 1851. [Census]

DE LATTE, or DALLET, WILLIAM, a weaver in Picardy, Edinburgh, grandson and heir of John De Latte or Dallet a weaver there, 1798. [NAS.NG1.66.6]

DE MEE, JOHN, a deed, 1697. [NAS.RD4.81.604/731]

DE MULLANDER, FRANCIS, a merchant in Bruges, 1686. [NAS.AC7.7]

DENNISTOUN, GEORGINA D., 14 Rue Monsieur le Prince, Paris, administration, 12 August 1892. [NAS.SC70/6]

DE PONTAC, Sir JOHN, seigneur de la Tour, husband of Margaret Pallotte, daughter of Peter Pallotte, a merchant in Bordeaux, a deed, 1692. [NAS.RD3.78.145]

DE RAMEZAY, CLAUDE, was descended from a Scottish family, named Ramsay, which had settled in Burgundy in the late 15th or early 16th century. Claude de Ramezay born 1659 in Burgundy, to Canada in 1685 as a soldier, acting governor of New France from 1714 to 1716, died in Quebec during 1724. [DCB.II.545]

DESABRIS, BENJAMIN, born in Rouen, France, around 1819, a cook in Edinburgh, 1851. [Census]

DESBOIERT, DESLIS, a French Protestant refugee in Edinburgh, a deed, 1697. [NAS.RD4.80.1061]

DE VENA, EUGENE F.M.J., born in France during 1806, a portrait painter in Edinburgh, 1851. [Census]

DE VERLAND, CHARLES, a French teacher at Perth Academy in 1797. [NAS.B59.24.6.115/125]

DE VILLE, ANDRE, born in Anjou, from France to Britain in 1790, a French teacher in Edinburgh, residing in St James Square, Edinburgh, in 1794. [ECA.SL115.1.1]

DICK, AGNES LOUISE, in Boulogne-sur-Mer, an inventory, 1877. [NAS.SC70.183/16]

DINGWALL, DANIEL, born 1716, a glover from Inverness, a Jacobite in 1745, transported from Liverpool on the Veteran bound for the Leeward Islands on 5 May 1747, liberated and landed on Martinique in June 1747. [P.2.154][NA.SP.36.102]

DONALD, JAMES, born 1727, a tailor in Mearns, a Jacobite in 1745, transported from Liverpool on the Veteran bound for the Leeward Islands on 5 May 1747, liberated and landed on Martinique in June 1747. [P.2.156][NA.SP.36.102][MR23]

DONALDSON, ALEXANDER, MD, in Paris, 1679, in Sedan, France, 1684, deeds. [NAS.RD4.46.335; RD3.60.104]

DONALDSON, JAMES, a student at Rheims University, 1722. [RCPE]

DONALDSON, JOSEPH, born in Glasgow, an author, died in Paris on 5 October 1830. [S#1144]

DOUGALL, JOHN, the younger, a merchant in France, 1642. [NAS.GD18.2416]

DOUGLAS, Lord GEORGE, Colonel of a Scottish regiment in France, 1560s. [NAS.NRAS.0.13]

DOUGLAS, Lord GEORGE, Colonel of the Old Scots Regiment in France, 1665. [NAS.RD4.14.209]

DOUGLAS, GEORGE, from Edinburgh, a student at Rheims University, 1727. [RCPE]

DOUGLAS, JAMES, born 1617, son of William, Earl of Angus, Colonel of a Scots regiment formerly commanded by Sir John Hepburn, killed at Douai on 21 October 1645. [SP.I.204]

DOUGLAS, JAMES, a student at Rheims University, 1684. [RCPE]

DOUGLAS, JAMES, a student at Rheims University, 1699. [RCPE]

DOUGLAS, JOHN, a Lieutenant of the Earl of Dunfermline's Regiment in France, 1676. [NAS.RD4.39.200]

DOUGLAS, WILLIAM, an officer of *Le Regiment Royal Ecossais*, 1744. [JAHR]

DRUET, JEAN, born in Nantes, France, a seaman aboard the Brave off St Domingo, a prisoner of war in Greenlaw, Scotland, died there 11 October 1811.
[NA.ADM.103/157/93; 103/117/92; 103/624; 103/648]

DRUMMOND, ANDREW, son of the Duke of Melfort, a student at the Scots College at Douai, 1694. [RSC.I.62]

DRUMMOND, CHARLES, born 1681, son of the Duke of Perth, a student at the Scots College at Douai, 1693. [RSC.I.62]

DRUMMOND, JAMES, born 1674, son of James Drummond, Earl of Perth, and his wife Jane Douglas, a Jacobite who fled to France in February 1716, died in Paris on 17 April 1720. [JP#146][SP.VII.54]

DRUMMOND, JAMES, born 1682, son of Ludovic
Drummond, a student at the Scots College at Douai,
1693, and at the Scots College in Paris from 1702 to
1704. [RSC.I.62][SCP.213]

DRUMMOND, JOHN, born 1679, son of the Duke of Perth, a
student at the Scots College at Douai, 1693. [RSC.I.62]

DRUMMOND, JOHN, graduated MD from Rheims
University in 1704. [NAS.NRAS.726.3.10]

DRUMMOND, JOHN, graduated MD from Rheims
University in 1723. [NAS.NRAS.726.3.43]

DRUMMOND, Lord JOHN, Colonel of *Le Regiment Royal
Ecossais*, 1744. [JAHR]

DRUMMOND, JOHN, an officer of *Le Regiment Royal
Ecossais*, 1744; a Captain of *Le Regiment d'Albanie*,
1748. [JAHR]

DRUMMOND, JOHN, a Lieutenant of *Le Regiment Royal
Ecossais*, 1756-1759. [JAHR]

DRUMMOND, LOUIS, an officer of *Le Regiment Royal
Ecossais*, 1744. [JAHR]

DRUMMOND, PHILLIP, a student at the Scots College at
Douai, 1700. [RSC.I.60]

DRUMMOND, REGINALD, a student at the Scots College at
Douai, 1700. [RSC.I.65]

DRUMMOND, WILLIAM, an officer of *Le Regiment Royal
Ecossais*, 1744. [JAHR]

DRUMMOND of STRATHALLAN, ..., an officer of *Le
Regiment Royal Ecossais*, 1744. [JAHR]

DRUMMOND, ..., Adjutant of the 67th Regiment, died in St
Domingo, 1796. [NAS.GD188.28.6]

DU BOSCQ, JOHN, a merchant in Bordeaux, a deed of factory, 1681. [NAS.RD3.49.453]

DU CORNETT, JAMES, a merchant in Bordeaux, a bond, 25 November 1661. [NAS.RD4.3.798; GD18.2408]

DUDDINGSTON, ELIZABETH, 58 Rue Jacob, Paris, will, 19 June 1866. [NAS.SC70/6]

DUFF, DANIEL, born 1721, a laborer in Perthshire, a Jacobite in 1745, transported from Liverpool on the Veteran bound for the Leeward Islands on 5 May 1747, liberated and landed on Martinique in June 1747. [P.2.168][NA.SP.36.102][MR206]

DUGUID, ALEXANDER, in Auchinhove, son of Francis Duguid of Auchinhove and his wife Teresa Leslie, a Jacobite and Lieutenant of Glenbucket's Regiment, fought at Sheriffmuir in 1715, fled to France in 1716. [JAB.54]

DUGUID, CHARLES, a student at Douai, 1756. [RSC.I.90]

DUGUID, HENRY, born 1748, son of Patrick Duguid baron of Auchenhove and Aemilia Irvine, a student at Douai, 1760. [RSC.I.92]

DUGUID, JAMES, son of Patrick Duguid baron of Auchenhove and Aemilia Irvine, a student at Douai, 1751. [RSC.I.88]

DUGUID, PATRICK, a student at Douai, 1765. [RSC.I.92]

DUN, WILLIAM, a student at Montpellier University, 1655. [RCPE]

DUNBAR, JAMES, born 1730, a labourer in Morayshire, a Jacobite in 1745, transported from Liverpool on the Veteran bound for the Leeward Islands on 5 May 1747, liberated and landed on Martinique in June 1747. [P.2.170][NA.SP.36.102]

DUNCAN, JAMES, born in Aberdeen, Scotland, a soldier of *Le Regiment d'Ogilvie*, 1762. [JAHR]

DUNCAN, WILLIAM, a sergeant of the 4th Regiment of Foot, in Guadaloupe, testament, 1762, Comm. Edinburgh. [NAS]

DUNDAS, ALEXANDER, graduated MD from Rheims University in 1695. [NAS.NRAS.726.3.2]

DUNDAS, ..., Colonel of the 82nd Regiment, died in St Domingo, 1796. [NAS.GD188.28.6]

DUNDASS, ..., a student at the Scots College at Douai, 1686. [RSC.I.59]

DUNLOP, LEONARD HILL, a merchant in St Vincent, son of James Dunlop in Glasgow, died in Guadaloupe during 1810. [EA#4844]

DURAGE, JOHN, in Bordeaux, a deed, 1767. [NAS.RD4.210/1.655]

DURIER, JEAN LOUIS, a French teacher in Edinburgh, died 29 December 1843, inventory, 1844, Comm. Edinburgh. [NAS]

DU VAL, JOSIAS, a factor in Le Havre, 1686. [NAS.AC7.8]

DYKES, MARGARET, born 1725, from Linlithgow, West Lothian, a Jacobite in 1745, transported from Liverpool on the Veteran bound for the Leeward Islands on 5 May 1747, liberated and landed on Martinique in June 1747. [P.2.154][NA.SP.36.102]

ECHLIN, DAVID, from Fife, a student at Montpellier University, 1606, and at Caen University, 1613. [RCPE]

ECCLES, WILLIAM, a student at Rheims University, 1684. [RCPE]

EDGAR, JOHN, son of Alexander Edgar and his wife Margaret Skinner, a Jacobite Life Guard in 1745, attempted to flee to America but was captured at sea by a French privateer and taken to France where he was commissioned in Ogilvy's Regiment in French Service, died in Scotland on 4 April 1788. [JP#249]

EDWARD, ANDREW, born 25 April 1722, a servant in Kirriemuir, Angus, a Jacobite in 1745, transported from Liverpool on the Veteran bound for the Leeward Islands on 5 May 1747, liberated and landed on Martinique in June 1747. [P.2.176][NA.SP.36.102][MR99]

ERNAULT, STEPHEN, a merchant and factor in Rouen, was admitted as a burgess and guilds-brother of Ayr in 1686, [ABR]; deeds, 1679, 1686, 1688, 1689. [NAS.RD4.45.166; RD4.58.740; RD2.68.43; RD64.17; RD3.70.256]

ERSKINE, JOHN, born in February 1675, son of Charles Erskine, Duke of Mar, and his wife Mary Maule, a Jacobite who fled via Montrose to St Malo, France, in 1716, died at Aix-la-Chapelle in May 1732. [JP#114][StAUL.Cheape.pp.5/537]

ERSKINE, MARIANNE, second daughter of John Francis Erskine, 12th Earl of Mar, died in Paris on 17 April 1844. [W.V.455]

ERSKINE, PATRICK, a student at Rheims University, 1738. [RCPE]

ERSKINE, WILLIAM, born 1688, son of William Erskine of Pittodrie and his wife Mary Grant, a Jacobite in 1715, settled in Bordeaux by 1719, died in February 1774. [JAB.60][CRA.82]

ESCLAPION, ANTHONY, a mariner on the Happy Amede of Martego, 1714. [NAS.RD4.89.348]

EVERTSTON, PETER, master of the St Michael of Calais, 1630. [NAS.AC7.2.291]

FAIR, GEORGE, a factor in Bordeaux, his relict Marion Davie, 1676. [NAS.GD172/366]

FAIRHOLM, THOMAS, a merchant in St Martins, was admitted as a burgess of St Andrews on 30 March 1738. [SABR]

FAIRLEY, THOMAS, born 1800, died in Marseilles on 4 May 1855. [Culross MI]

FALCONER, ARCHIBALD, born 1674, from Edinburgh, a student at the Scots College at Douai, 1688. [RSC.I.60]

FALCONER, CHARLES, a student at Rheims University, 1699. [RCPE]

FALL, JAMES, in Paris, 1681. [NAS.GD406.1.6193]

FANSON, PHILLIP, a merchant in Angoulme on the Charente River, 1680. [NAS.AC7.5]

FANSON, THEODORE, a merchant in Angoulme on the Charente River, 1680. [NAS.AC7.5]

FARQUHARSON, CHARLES, of Balmoral, son of William Farquharson of Inverey and his wife Agnes Gordon, a Jacobite army major at the Battle of Killiecrankie in 1689, later an agent in France, died in 1718. [JAB.66]

FARQUHARSON, CHARLES, from Banff, graduated MD from Rheims University, 1751. [RCPE]

FARQUHARSON, JOHN, Principal of the Scots College at Douai from 1785 to 1793. [NLS.Adv.ms29.3,16/44]

s
FARQUHARSON, PETER, of Inverey, son of John Farquharson of Inverey and his wife Margaret Gordon, Jacobite Colonel of Mar's Regiment at the Battle of Sherifmuir, fled to France in 1716, died in Scotland during 1737. [JAB.62][CRA.54]

FARQUHARSON, WILLIAM, son of Henry Farquharson of Whitehouse, Aberdeen, graduated MD from Rheims University in 1751. [RCPE]

FARQUHARSON, ..., a Lieutenant of *Le Regiment Royal Ecossais,* 1756-1760. [JAHR]

FEA, ALEXANDER, a prisoner in Edinburgh Tolbooth, released to go to France as a soldier on 4 February 1676. [RPCS.3/1V.668]

FEA, JOHN, a prisoner in Edinburgh Tolbooth, released to go to France as a soldier on 4 February 1676. [RPCS.3/1V.668]

FEA, ROBERT, a prisoner in Edinburgh Tolbooth, released to go to France as a soldier on 4 February 1676. [RPCS.3/1V.668]

FERGUSON, DAVID, at Pointe Petre, Guadaloupe, 1784. [ASS#125/767]

FERRIER, DAVID, a Captain of *Le Regiment d'Ogilvie,* 1747. [JAHR]

FERVAGNE, JEAN NICOLAS, born in Amiens, France, a soldier of the 26th Regiment, captured in Martinique, a prisoner of war in Valleyfield, Scotland, died there on 10 May 1814. [NAS.Adm.list 1821/110; NA.ADM.103.435/4372, 103.648]

FLAHAULT, AUGUSTE CHARLES JOSEPH, Count de, Rue de Lille, Paris, an inventory, 1871. [NAS.SC70.151/ 257]

FLEMING, CHARLES, born 1675, son of William Fleming, 5th Earl of Wigtown, and Henrietta Seton, educated at the Scots College in Paris in 1687, and at the Scots College at Douai in 1689, died in Cumbernauld on 16 May 1747. [NAS.CH1.2.5][SCP.211][RSC.I.60]

FLEMING, MALCOLM, graduated MD from Rheims University, 1724. [RCPE]

FLETCHER, ROBERT, the younger, of Ballinshoe, Kirriemuir, Angus, Jacobite Major of Ogilvy's Regiment in 1745, fled via Dundee to Norway, Sweden, and finally

France in 1746, a Captain of *Le Regiment d'Ogilvie*, 1747. [JAHR][OR1/127][LPR#210][LPR.210][GK#113]

FONTAINE, EDWARD, graduated MD from Rheims University, 1705. [RCPE]

FORBES, ARTHUR, graduated MD from Rheims University, 1686. [RCPE]

FORBES, Sir ARTHUR, of Craigievar, died in Boulogne-sur-Mer on 27 February 1823. [SM.86/520]

FORBES, CHARLES, son of Arthur Forbes of Brux, Kildrummy, Aberdeenshire, and his wife Elizabeth Murray, a Jacobite in 1715 who fled to France. [JAB.77][CRA.125]

FORBES, CHARLES, born 1742, a student at Douai, 1752. [RSC.I.89]

FORBES, JAMES, graduated MD from Rheims University, 1724. [RCPE]

FORBES, JOHN, from Morayshire, graduated MD from Rheims University, 1713. [RCPE]

FORBES, JOHN, from Edinburgh, graduated MD from Rheims University, 1729. [RCPE]

FORBES, JOHN, from Fife, graduated MD from Rheims University, 1731. [RCPE]

FORBES, JOHN, a Captain of *Le Regiment d'Ogilvie*, 1759. [JAHR]

FORBES, NATHANIEL, of Ardgeith, son of George Forbes of Skellatur, a Jacobite and a Major of Mar's Regiment, captured at the Siege of Preston on 13 November 1715, imprisoned in London but escaped via Holland to France in 1718. [JAB.86][CRA.181]

FORBES, PATRICK, graduated MD from Rheims University, 1713. [RCPE]

FORBES, ROBERT, born 1739, a student at Douai, 1753.
[RSC.I.89]

FORBES, THOMAS, a Lieutenant of the Scots Guards of
France, 1560s. [NAS.NRAS.0.143]

FORBES, THOMAS, of Tolquhoun, born in 1689, son of
Thomas Forbes of Little Auchry and his wife Henrietta
Erskine, a Jacobite in 1715 who fled to France, died in
London in 1728. [JAB.87/217][CRA.185]

FORBES of SKELLATUR, ..., a Captain of *Le Regiment
d'Ogilvie*, 1747. [JAHR]

FORBES of FILLERY, ..., a Captain of Grenadiers in *Le
Regiment d'Ogilvie*, 1747-1756. [JAHR]

FORDYCE, or BALFOUR, EUPHEMIA KATHERINE,
died in Pu Basse, Pyrenees, on 9 January 1852.
[Markinch, Fife, MI]

FORTOLIS, FRANCOIS, a mariner on the Happy Amede of
Martego, 1714. [NAS.RD4.89.348]

FOTHERINGHAM, ALEXANDER, from Edinburgh,
graduated MD from Rheims University in 1751. [RCPE]

FOTHERINGHAM, ROBERT, graduated MD from Rheims
University in 1745. [RCPE]

FOTHERINGHAM, THOMAS, a Captain of *Le Regiment
d'Ogilvie*, 1747. [JAHR]

FOULIS, DAVID, graduated MD from Rheims University,
1735. [RCPE][NAS.NRAS.726.3.59]

FOULIS, THOMAS, a merchant in St Sebastian and
Bordeaux, 1639. [NAS.GD18/2371]

FRANCE, JACOB, a merchant in St Martin's, was admitted
as a burgess and guilds-brother of Ayr on 22 May 1683.
[ABR]

FRASER, DAVID, in Martinique, 1799. [SA#260]

FRASER, JOHN, son of William Fraser and Margaret McDonald, a student at Douai, 1742. [RSC.I.85]

FRASER, MARGARET, born 1772, second wife of David George Sandeman of Springfield, died in Bordeaux on 4 July 1835. [Perth, Greyfriars, MI]

FRASER, PETER, educated at the Scots College in Paris from 1696 to 1702, ordained at Scothouse on 11 March 1704, a priest in Strathaven, Banffshire, 1710, died at Morar on 9 March 1731. [NAS.CH1.2.30/1/5][SCP.212]

FRASER, SIMON, a Jacobite Captain who was captured at the Siege of Preston in 1715 but escaped to France. [JAB.92]

FRASER of FAIRFIELD, ..., a Captain of *Le Regiment d'Albanie*, 1748. [JAHR]

FRASER, ..., Lieutenant of the 1st [Royal Scots] Regiment, died in St Domingo, 1796. [NAS.GD188.28.6]

FREELAND, JOHN, in Nice, an inventory, 1878. [NAS.SC70.187/710]

FULLARTON, JOHN, of Dudwick, son of Robert Udny and Elizabeth Fullarton, a Jacobite who fought at Sheriffmuir in 1715, later fled via Banff to Norway, Hamburg, Holland and finally France. [JAB.93][NA.SP35.7.75][CRA.191]

FULLERTON, WILLIAM, graduated MD from Rheims University, 1719. [RCPE]

GALT, ARCHIBALD, a factor in Bordeaux, around 1700. [NAS.CS96.3309]

GARDYNE of LAYTON, ..., a Captain of *Le Regiment d'Ogilvie*, 1747. [JAHR]

GARROW, WILLIAM, from Banff, graduated MD from Rheims University in 1751. [RCPE]

GAUTER, PETER, a French hatter in Edinburgh, husband of Jean Thomson, a deed, 1700. [NAS.RD4.86.714]

GEDDES, ALEXANDER, born 1737 at Pathhead near Preshome, son of Alexander Geddes and Janet Mitchell, educated at the Scots College in Paris 1758, ordained in Paris 1764, died in London on 20 February 1802. [SCP.218]

GEDDES, CHARLES, of the Scots Guards of France, 1560s. [NAS.NRAS.0.143]

GENODEAU, JEAN, born in Nantes, a seaman aboard the Gerf in the West Indies, a prisoner of war in Greenlaw, Scotland, died there 14 March 1808. [NA.ADM.103.155/104, 103.624, 103.648]

GERAULT, BERTRAND, a merchant in Bordeaux, 1686. [NAS.AC7.7]

GHIMAR, LOUIS, born in Brussels around 1821, a lithographer and artist, with Henrietta Ghimar, born in Brussels around 1823, and Sophie Ghimar, born in Brussels around 1826, in Edinburgh, 1851. [Census]

GIBB, ALEXANDER NEWLANDS, in Toulouse, an inventory, 1871. [NAS.SC70.154/78]

GIBBS, FREDERICK, from Dunfermline, a student at Orange University, 1665. [RCPE]

GILCHRIST, Dr JOHN BORTHWICK, in Paris, formerly on Honorable East India Company Service, died 8 January 1841, inventory, 1841, Comm. Edinburgh. [NAS][W#/107]

GILCHRIST, ..., Deputy Commissary General, St Domingo, 1796. [NAS.GD188.28.6]

GILMOUR, Sir CHARLES, died in France on 9 August 1750. [NAS.GD122.4.19]

GIROT, ETIENNE, born in Toulon, France, a seaman aboard the Duquesne, captured off St Domingo, a prisoner of war in Jamaica later in Greenlaw, Scotland, died there 6 August 1808. [NA.ADM.103.155/129, 103.624, 103.648]

GLASS, Mr ROBERT, a merchant in Bordeaux, was admitted as a burgess and guilds-brother of Ayr on 1 July 1721. [ABR]

GLEN, THOMAS, graduated MD from Rheims University, 1726; 1759. [RCPE][NAS.NRAS.726.3.92]

GLENDINNING, CHARLES, born 1746, a student at the Scots College at Douai, 1759. [RSC.I.91]

GLENDINNING, JAMES, born 7 September 1744, a student at the Scots College at Douai, 1757. [RSC.I.90]

GLENDINNING, ROBERT, son of Robert Glendinning and Mary Nelson, a student at Douai, 1750. [RSC.I.87]

GLESFORD, JOHN, in Martinique, 1799. [SA#260]

GONZALES, JOSEPH, born in France around 1824, a clerk of the General Post Office in Edinburgh, 1851. [Census]

GOLYINYOW, ISAAC, a French pirate imprisoned in Dunbar Tolbooth, 1630. [NAS.AC7.2.362]

GOODBRAND, ALEXANDER, born 1717, a carpenter in Banff, a Jacobite in 1745, transported from Liverpool on the Veteran bound for the Leeward Islands on 5 May 1747, liberated and landed on Martinique in June 1747. [P.2.232][NA.SP.36.102][JAB.2.428]

GORDON, ALEXANDER, from Banff, graduated MD from Rheims University, 1701. [RCPE]

GORDON, ALEXANDER, a merchant in St Martins, France, 1726, 1740. [SIL#258] [NAS.RS29.6.468]

GORDON, ALEXANDER, a merchant and factor in
Bordeaux, and Katherine Kinloch a marriage contract,
1730; was admitted as a burgess of St Andrews on 5
August 1730. [SAU: Burgh Court Book]; 1740; later a
merchant in Boulogne-sur- Mer, died around 1756.
[NAS.RD3.210.46; RS29.6.413; NA17313]

GORDON, ALEXANDER, merchant in France, testament,
1750, Commissary of Edinburgh. [NAS]

GORDON, ALEXANDER, a merchant in Boulogne –sur-
Mer, around 1774, uncle of Mary Shirras or Farquhar in
Gilcomston, see testament, 7 October 1774, Comm.
Aberdeen. [NAS]

GORDON, Dr ANDREW, in Santa Cruz, Martinique, letters,
1763-1767. [NAS.NRAS.96/18]

GORDON, ANNA, sister of George, Duke of Gordon, and
spouse of Sir Miles O'Cruily, commandant of the
"English Gens d'Armes" in France, a deed, 1688.
[NAS.RD3.67.422]

GORDON, CATHERINE, born 1804, daughter of William
Gordon and his wife Margaret Stuart, died in Paris on 18
December 1883. [Bellie Tynet MI]

GORDON, DAVID, in Martinique, 1799. [SA#260]

GORDON, FRANCIS, born 1742, son of ....Gordon of
Kenmore, a student at Douai, 1751. [RSC.I.88]

GORDON, Lord GEORGE, Captain in Chief of a company
of Men at Arms of Louis XIII of France, 13 March 1625.
[NAS.RH1/2/447]

GORDON, GEORGE, graduated MD from Rheims
University, 1657. [RCPE]

GORDON, GEORGE, born 1675, a student at the Scots
College at Douai, 1685. [RSC.I.58]

GORDON, GEORGE, son of J. Gordon of Beldormie and Mary Gordon, a student at the Scots College in Paris from 1735 to 1742, later an apprentice ship-carpenter in Leith. [SCP.216]

GORDON, GEORGE, a factor at Rouan, testament, 1743, Commissary of Edinburgh. [NAS]

GORDON, GEORGE, from Aberdeen, graduated MD from Rheims University, 1687. [RCPE]

GORDON, JAMES, from Banff, graduated MD from Rheims University, 1706. [RCPE]

GORDON, JAMES, from Aberdeen, graduated MD from Rheims University, 1728. [RCPE]

GORDON, JAMES, of Auchleuchries, died at the Scots College in Paris on 3 September 1762. [SCP.I.218]

GORDON, JAMES FARQUHAR, Writer to the Signet, died in Avranches, Normandy, on 23 December 1843. [AJ#5009]

GORDON, JOHN, a student at the Scots College at Douai, 1685. [RSC.I.58]

GORDON, JOHN, HM chaplain in New York, Episcopal Bishop of Galloway 1688, settled in Ireland during 1689, later moved to France, chaplain at the Jacobite Court at St Germains. [Keith#283]

GORDON, JOHN, son of Adam Gordon of Balgowan, a Jacobite who fled abroad via Banff in 1716, settled in Rouen, France. [JAB.97][CRA.116]

GORDON, JOHN, born 1728, a weaver in Loynavere, Elgin, Morayshire, a Jacobite in 1745, transported from Liverpool on the <u>Veteran</u> bound for the Leeward Islands on 5 May 1747, liberated and landed on Martinique in June 1747. [P.2.238][NA.SP.36.102][MR123]

GORDON, JOHN, born 1824, of Charleston and Kinnaber, by Montrose, Angus, died in Pau on 20 January 1862. [Kinnaber MI]

GORDON, PATRICK, from Montrose, graduated MD from Rheims University, 1719. [RCPE]

GORDON, ROBERT, a merchant in Bordeaux, was admitted as a burgess and guilds-brother of Glasgow in 1714; a factor in Bordeaux pre-1720s. [GBR][NAS.RH15.32.21; GD96.3074; RD4.100.231]

GORDON, ROBERT, of Hallhead, sometime a wine-merchant in Bordeaux during 1720s; thereafter in Edinburgh, testament, 1737, Commissary of Edinburgh. [NAS.NRAS.2362/316]

GORDON, ROBERT, son of the late Alexander Gordon, a merchant in Boulogne sur Mer, testament, 1759, Commissary of Edinburgh. [NAS]

GORDON, THOMAS, a student at Caen University, 1677. [RCPE]

GORDON, THOMAS, graduated MD from Rheims University, 1724. [RCPE]

GORDON, WILLIAM, a merchant in Edinburgh, formerly a factor in Paris, deeds, 1702, 1705, 1707. [NAS.RD4.90.532; RD4.97.619/973; RD4.100.412]

GORDON, WILLIAM, from Aberdeen, graduated MD from Rheims University, 1719. [RCPE]

GORDON, ..., an infantry captain, from France to Louisiana on the Count de Toulouse, Captain le Chevalier de Grieu, in 1718. [NWI.1.473]

GORDON of CARNOUSIE, ..., a Captain of *Le Regiment d'Ogilvie*, 1747. [JAHR]

GORDON, ..., Lieutenant of the 67th Regiment, died in St Domingo, 1796. [NAS.GD188.28.6]

GOULD, EDMUND, a merchant in La Rochelle, deeds, 1682.
[NAS.RD2.57.544; RD3.51.479; RD3.53.151]

GORDON, ..., quartermaster of the 6th West India Regiment,
died in St Domingo, 1796. [NAS.GD188.28.6]

GRAEME, GEORGE, graduated MD from Rheims
University, 1701. [RCPE]

GRAEME, HUGH, former Naval Officer of Guadaloupe,
1765; testament, 1769, Commissary of Edinburgh.
[NAS.RD4.197/2.559]

GRAEME, WILLIAM ALEXIS, from Edinburgh, a student
at Montpellier University, 1709. [RCPE]

GRAEME, WILLIAM, graduated MD from Rheims
University, 1722. [RCPE]

GRAHAM, JAMES, graduated MD from Rheims University,
1718. [RCPE]

GRAHAM, JAMES, of Airth, a Captain of *Le Regiment
d'Albanie*, 1748. [JAHR]

GRAHAM, PATRICK, son of Colonel Peter Graham, a
student at the Scots College at Douai, 1696. [RSC.I.64]

GRAHAM, PETER, ..., a Captain of *Le Regiment d'Albanie*,
1748. [JAHR]

GRAHAM, ROBERT, of Garrig, a Captain of *Le Regiment
d'Albanie*, 1748. [JAHR]

GRAHAM, THOMAS, an archer of the Scots Guards of
France, 1560s. [NAS.NRAS.0.143]

GRAHAM, THOMAS, graduated MD from Rheims
University, 1714. [RCPE]

GRAHAM, WALTER, graduated MD from Rheims
University, 1722. [RCPE]

GRAHAM, WILLIAM, graduated MD from Rheims University, 1727. [NAS.NRAS.726.3.52; 4.5]

GRAHAM of DUNDEE, Viscount, a Captain of *Le Regiment d'Ogilvie*, 1747. [JAHR]

GRALEICK, ANTONIE, born in France around 1809, a cook in Edinburgh, 1851. [Census]

GRAME, JOHN, a Lieutenant of Grenadiers in *Le Regiment d'Ogilvy*, 1760. [JAHR]

GRANDE, SCIPIO, a mariner on the Happy Amede of Martego, 1701. [NAS.RD4.89.348]

GRANT, ALEXANDER, born 1680, son of William Grant of Crichy, a student at the Scots College at Douai, 1693. [RSC.I.62]

GRANT, ALEXANDER, born 1722, a carpenter in Aberdeen, a Jacobite in 1745, transported from Liverpool on the Veteran bound for the Leeward Islands on 5 May 1747, liberated and landed on Martinique in June 1747. [P.2.250][NA.SP.36.102][JAB.2.429][MR.127]

GRANT, CHARLES, born 1728, a miller in Abernethy, Inverness-shire, a Jacobite in 1745, transported from Liverpool on the Veteran bound for the Leeward Islands on 5 May 1747, liberated and landed on Martinique in June 1747. [P.2.252][NA.SP.36.102][MR206]

GRANT, CHARLOTTE LOUISA, youngest daughter of Robert Grant of Tillyfour, Aberdeen, died in Rue de Rivoli, Paris, on 2 August 1839. [EEC#19934][AJ#4774]

GRANT, EUPHEMIA, daughter of Lieutenant Edward Grant of the Royal Navy, who died on 6 November 1857, of Rockhouse, Lossiemouth, Morayshire, and his wife Margaret Nicol who died in January 1848, and wife of Reverend Louis A. Sery of the French National Reformed Church. [NAS.SH.1861]

GRANT, GEORGE, from Morayshire, graduated MD from Rheims University, 1753. [RCPE]

GRANT, GREGORY, graduated MD from Rheims University, 1757. [NAS.NRAS.726.3.89]

GRANT, JOHN, born 15 August 1672, son of Peter Grant of Caron and .... Dunbar, a student at the Scots College at Douai, 1695. [RSC.I.63]

GRANT, JOHN, born 1685, son of John Grant of Ballindalloch, a student at the Scots College at Douai, 1695. [RSC.I.64]

GRANT, JOHN, born 1707, a laborer from Inverness-shire, a Jacobite in 1745, transported from Liverpool on the Veteran bound for the Leeward Islands on 5 May 1747, liberated and landed on Martinique in June 1747. [P.2.260][NA.SP.36.102][MR35]

GRANT, JOHN, a student at Douai, 1748. [RSC.I.86]

GRANT, MALCOLM, 46 Rue du President, Ixelles, Bruxelles, will, 8 March 1879. [NAS.SC70/6]

GRANT, PATRICK, in Martinique, 1763. [NAS.GD248.521.3/5]
GRANT, ..., a Captain of *Le Regiment d'Ogilvie,* 1747. [JAHR]

GRAY, ALEXANDER, graduated MD from Rheims University, 1780. [RCPE]

GRAY, JOHN, a Captain of *Le Regiment Royal Ecossais,* 1744-1761. [JAHR]

GRAY, WILLIAM, from Montrose, a student at Montpellier University, 1611, and at Orange University, 1614. [RCPE]

GREGORY, DAVID, a merchant in Dunkirk, 1764; a letter, 1785. [NAS.GD80.656; GD503.135]

GUILLEAUME, PETER, died on 27 August 1831 aged 29, Clement Villeneauve Guilleaume died 30 May 1824 aged 6 weeks, Henry Peter Guilleaume died 14 January 1827 aged 1 year 5 months, and Helen Marret Guilleaume died 5 July 1842. [Montrose, Angus, MI]

GUIRAUD, BERTRAND, a merchant in Bordeaux, deeds, 1686, 1687. [NAS.RD3.64.379; RD4.58.467; RD3.66.153]

GUNN, JESSIE, wife of James Roger in Dunkirk, heir to her mother Isabel Wilkie who died on 4 August 1869, widow of John Gunn there, 5 March 1869. [NAS.S/H]

GUTHRIE, JAMES, Assistant Quarter Master General in Jeremie, Haiti, 1796-1798. [NAS.GD188.box 28.28.1]

GUTHRIE, JOHN, from Edinburgh, a student at Orange University, 1658. [RCPE]

HAGGARSTON, MARGARET FRANCES, wife of Lewis Eyre in Brussels, heir to her great great grandfather William Robertson of Ladykirk who died on 25 April 1783, 28 December 1852. [NAS.Services of Heirs]

HAGGARSTON, WINIFRED, a nun in St Andres Convent in Belgium, heir to her great great grandfather William Robertson of Ladykirk who died on 25 April 1783, 28 December 1852. [NAS.Services of Heirs]

HAIG, WILLIAM, son of James Antony Haig and his wife Barbara Robertson, died in Martinique during 1794. [Haig of Bemersyde pedigree]

HALDANE, PATRICK, graduated MD from Rheims University, 1758. [NAS.NRAS.726.3.91]

HALIBURTON, JOHN, a merchant in Dunkirk, 1764, in Edinburgh by 1782, graduated MD from Rheims University, 1718. [RCPE]

HALIBURTON, PATRICK, graduated MD from Rheims University, 1680. [RCPE]

HALKET, CHARLES, born 1727, a laborer in Aberdeen, a Jacobite in 1745, transported from Liverpool on the Veteran bound for the Leeward Islands on 5 May 1747, liberated and landed on Martinique in June 1747. [P.2.272][NA.SP.36.102][JAB.2.430][MR9]

HALL, ANDREW, graduated MD from Rheims University, 1717. [RCPE]

HALL, AUGUSTUS, graduated MD from Rheims University, 1713. [RCPE]

HALL, WILLIAM, in Rouen, 1748, of the Hall of Dunglass, East Lothian family. [NAS.GD206.2.520]

HAMILTON, ALEXANDER, a merchant in Rouen, husband of Janet Kirkland, deeds, 1684, 1685. [NAS.RD2.59.454/464; RD4.57.440]

HAMILTON, ALEXANDER, born 12 December 1767, fifth son of Dunbar Hamilton of Baldoon and his wife Helen Hamilton, an officer of the 38th Regiment of Foot, died in Guadaloupe in June 1794. [SP.VII.522]

HAMILTON, DAVID, from Glasgow, graduated MD from Rheims University, 1686. [RCPE][NAS.NRAS.332.M11.59]

HAMILTON, ELIZABETH, born 1725, a seamstress in Banff, a Jacobite in 1745, transported from Liverpool on the Veteran bound for the Leeward Islands on 5 May 1747, liberated and landed on Martinique in June 1747. [P.2.118][NA.SP.36.102][JAB.2.422]

HAMILTON, ISOBEL, born 1697, a knitter in Musselburgh, Midlothian, a Jacobite in 1745, transported from Liverpool on the Veteran bound for the Leeward Islands on 5 May 1747, liberated and landed on Martinique in June 1747. [NA.SP.36.102]

HAMILTON, Reverend JAMES ALEXANDER, in Liege, heir to his father James Hamilton of Kames, Bute, Writer

Scots-French Links in Europe and America, 1550-1850

to the Signet, who died on 5 January 1849, 25 July 1854. [NAS.S/H]

HAMILTON, JOHN, an archer of the Scots Guards of France, 1560s. [NAS.NRAS.0.143]

HAMILTON, JOHN, ("Jean"), born 1714, son of John or Jean Hamilton and his wife Marie Hamilton, baptised on 2 August 1716 in the Church of St Jean Baptiste, Annapolis Royal, Acadia. [NSARM.RG1, Vol.26.143]

HAMILTON, SAMUEL, a factor in Rouen, 1676. [NAS.AC7.4]

HAMILTON, THOMAS, graduated MD from Rheims University, 1680. [RCPE]

HAMILTON, THOMAS, a merchant in Ostend, a bond, 1683. [NAS.RD4.52.419]

HAMILTON, WILLIAM, graduated MD from Rheims University, 1733. [RCPE]

HANNAY, JAMES, was admitted as a burgess of Glasgow on 27 September 1627 as he had gone as a soldier to aid in the relief of La Rochelle. [GBR]

HANSON, JACOB, master of the Hope of Calais, 1630. [NAS.AC7.1.259]

HARDIE, Dr JAMES, HEICS, died in Paris on 26 May 1834, inventory, 1838, Comm. Edinburgh. [NAS]

HARPER, JAMES, a merchant in Rouen, 1630. [NAS.RH9.5.8]

HARRIS, GORDON, an officer of *Le Regiment Royal Ecossais,* 1744. [JAHR]

HAY, ADAM, of Smithfield and Haystoun, born 1796, died in Cannes on 11 January 1867. [AJ#6211]

HAY, CHARLES, from Galloway, graduated MD from Rheims University, 1737. [RCPE]

HAY, GEORGE, in the kingdom of France, son to the late George Hay of Balhousie, testament, 28 August 1684, Comm. Dunblane. [NAS]

HAY, GEORGE, a skipper of Rouen, master of the George of Rouen, later known as the George of Leith, 1686. [NAS.AC7.7]

HAY, JAMES, graduated MD from Rheims University, 1714. [RCPE]

HAY, JOHN, of Cromlix, born 1691, son of the Earl of Perth, the Jacobite Governor of Perth, fled to France in 1716, settled at St Germains, died on 24 September 1740. [NAS.B59.30.6/35; SC20.36.7][JP.68][SP.V.231]

HAY, WILLIAM, from Edinburgh, graduated MD from Rheims University, 1738. [RCPE] [NAS.NRAS.726.3.65]

HAY, ..., an officer of *Le Regiment Royal Ecossais*, 1744. [JAHR]

HAY, ..., Captain of the 83rd Regiment, died in St Domingo, 1796. [NAS.GD188.28.6]

HEBERT, ANDREW, a merchant in Paris, a deed, 1700. [NAS.RD2.84.253]

HEDOUX, SIMON, master of the Lewda of Dunkirk, 1630. [NAS.AC7.1.259]

HENDERSON, CHARLES, in Edinburgh, sometime in St Brieux, Brittany, died 14 October 1832, inventory, 1833, Comm. Edinburgh. [NAS]

HENDERSON, JAMES, born 1717, a cook, a Jacobite soldier of Ogilvy's Regiment in 1745, transported from Liverpool on the Veteran bound for the Leeward Islands on 5 May 1747, liberated and landed on Martinique in June 1747. [P.2.282][OR31][NA.SP.36.102]

HENDERSON, JOHN, born 1768, son of John Henderson and his wife Elizabeth Hay, a Captain of the 42nd Regiment, died in Paullace on 7 July 1814. [Logie, Fife, MI]

HENDERSON, ..., a Captain of *Le Regiment Royal Ecossais*, 1745-1761. [JAHR]

HENDRIE, JAMES, a merchant tailor in Somers-en-Anjou, a deed, 1685. [NAS.RD2.66.345]

HEPBURN, JOHN, in Edinburgh, formerly at Chastillion, France, a deed, 1670. [NAS.RD2.28.505]

HEPBURN, PATRICK, a student at Montpellier University, 1611. [RCPE]

HERNANDEZ, RITA HERNANDEZ de ALBA de, in Le Havre, an inventory, 1872. [NAS.SC70.160/330]

HERRIES, JAMES, born 1753, son of Robert Herries of Auchenshun and Joan Douglas, a student at Douai, 1764. [RSC.1.92]

HEW, JAMES, was admitted as a burgess of Glasgow on 27 September 1627 as he had gone as a soldier to aid in the relief of La Rochelle. [GBR]

HIGGINS, JOHN, a merchant in Paris, bonds, 1683. [NAS.RD4.52.509-511]

HINCHELWOOD, WASHINGTON, in Paris, an inventory, 1879. [NAS.SC70.197/90]

HOLLAND, RALPH, merchant in Bordeaux, 1680. [NAS.RH15/106/387]

HOME, ALEXANDER, graduated MD from Rheims University, 1681. [RCPE]

HOME, ALEXANDER, graduated MD from Rheims University in 1695. [NAS.NRAS.726/3.4]

HOME, GEORGE, born 1717, a writer in Edinburgh, a Jacobite in 1745, transported from Liverpool on the Veteran bound for the Leeward Islands on 5 May 1747, liberated and landed on Martinique in June 1747. [NA.SP.36.102][P.2.290]

HOME, HENRY, of the Scots Guards of France, 1560s. [NAS.NRAS.0.143]

HONEYMAN, WILLIAM THOMSON, late of Havre de Grace, died 25 August 1828, inventory, 1828, Comm. Edinburgh. [NAS]

HOPE, Rear Admiral CHARLES, second son of the late Right Honourable Charles Hope, died in Trouville on 6 August 1854. [W.XV.1572]

HOPE, OLIVER, residing in France, descended from the Hopes of Craighall, genealogy, 18 June 1767. [NAS.Lyon Office]

HORSBURGH, DAVID, graduated MD from Rheims University, 1733; 1739. [RCPE][NAS.NRAS.726.3.64]

HOUSTON, JAMES, graduated MD from Rheims University, 1714; 1717. [RCPE][NAS.NRAS.726.3.33]

HUGHES, DAVID, a burgess of Paris, bonds, 1669, 1674, 1675. [NAS.RD4.25.72; RD4.35.823; RD4.36.566]

HUME, PATRICK, of Polwarth, a Covenanter refugee in Bordeaux, 1686. [NAS.GD158.1018, #9/10]

HUNTER, JOHN, from Perthshire, in Uccle near Brussels, died 12 July 1840, inventory, 1841, Comm. Edinburgh. [NAS]

HUTCHESON, DAVID, from Lothian, graduated MD from Rheims University, 1740. [RCPE]

HUTCHISON, SUSANNA CAMPBELL, in Paris, an inventory, 1878. [NAS.SC70.191/291]

HUTSON, ALEXANDER, in Paris, brother of Andrew Hutson a merchant burgess of Edinburgh, 1605. [RPCS.VII.75]

INGLIS, JOHN, a merchant burgess of Edinburgh, sometime in Bordeaux, 1652. [RGS.X.20]

INGLIS, WILLIAM, a student at the Scots College at Douai, 1685. [RSC.I.57]

INNES, JOHN, a merchant and writer in Edinburgh, trading with Bordeaux, between 1708 and 1721. [NAS.NA17295]

INNES, ROBERT, rector of the Scots College at Douai, 1752. [RSC.I.89]

INNES, WALTER, formerly prior of a convent in Burgundy, later in Drumgask, Scotland, 1714. [NLS.ms976.143]

IRELAND, JAMES, born 1800, a flax-spinner from Dundee, died in Wambreechies, near Lille, on 28 February 1864. [DPCA#4201]

IRVINE, ALEXANDER, (?), in Bordeaux, a letter, 1717. [NAS.RH1/2.940]

IRVINE, ALEXANDER, from Aberdeen, graduated MD from Rheims University, 1744. [RCPE]

IRVINE, MARIE, born 1626 in Scotland, fled to France as a Catholic, moved to Quebec in 1642, then in Dieppe, France, from 1643 to 1657, returned to New France as a nun in 1657, entered the Hotel Dieu. Died in Quebec on 14 November 1687. [DCB.I.382]

IRVING, ROBERT, a Captain of the King of France's Guards, 7 March 1656. [RGS.X.525]

IZATT, EDWARD, from Culross, a student at Rheims University, 1681. [RCPE]

JACKSON, WILLIAM, born on 28 April 1725, son of John Jackson and his wife Elizabeth Fife in Kettins, Angus, a labourer and a Jacobite soldier of Ogilvy's Regiment in 1745, transported from Liverpool on the Veteran bound for the Leeward Islands on 5 May 1747, liberated and landed on Martinique in June 1747. [P.2.200][OR33][NA.SP.36.102]

JAMART, JACOB, a merchant in Bordeaux, was admitted as a burgess and guilds-brother of Ayr on 29 May 1671. [ABR]

JANSEN, ALBERT, a skipper in Calais, master of the Jonas of Dunkirk, 1628. [NAS.AC7.1.190]

JANTELOTT, SIMEON, a merchant in St Foy, France, a bond, 1682. [NAS.RD4.51.180]

JAPP, JOHN, born 1731, a carpenter in Banff, a Jacobite in 1745, transported from Liverpool on the Veteran bound for the Leeward Islands on 5 May 1747, liberated and landed on Martinique in June 1747. [NA.SP.36.102] [JAB.2.431][P.2.302]

JOHNSON, ANDREW COCHRAN, son of the late Earl of Dundonald, married Amelia Constance Gertrude Etiennette de Clugny, only child of the late Baron de Clugny, Governor of Guadaloupe, and widow of Raymond Godet, in Martinique on 21 March 1803. [GM.73.689]

JOHNSTON, ALEXANDER, a silversmith in Dundee, a Jacobite Life Guard in 1745, fled via Dundee to Norway in 1746, imprisoned in Bergen, later settled in France. [LPR#218][OR127]

JOHNSTON, CHARLES, in Ostend, a merchant from Dumfries, testament 1793, Comm. Dumfries. [NAS]

JOHNSTON, JAMES, alias Chevalier de Johnston, born
1719, son of an Edinburgh merchant, a Jacobite Captain
in the Duke of Perth's Regiment, fought at the Battle of
Culloden in 1746, fled via Holland to France, joined the
French Army, sent to Canada, fought in the French and
Indian Wars, and at the Plains of Abraham, returned to
France, died around 1800. [P.

JOHNSTON, JAMES, a student at Douai, 1750. [RSC.I.87]

JOHNSTON, JOHN, a student at Caen University, 1671.
[RCPE]

JOHNSTON, WILLIAM, from Aberdeen, a student at Orange
University, 1622. [RCPE]

JOHNSTON, WILLIAM, born 1803, died in St Bartholemew,
French West Indies, on 21 November 1827. [St
Michael's, Dumfries, MI]

JOHNSTONE, WILLIAM, of Blacklaws, second son of
James Johnstone, Marquis of Annandale, and his wife
Margaret Douglas, a Lieutenant Colonel of the Douglas
Regiment in French Service, died at Newbie in 1656.
[SP.I.258]

JOHNSTON, ..., a Captain of Grenadiers in *Le Regiment
d'Ogilvie,* 1756. [JAHR]

JOINER, DAVID, born 1727, a Jacobite in Aberdeen, a
Jacobite in 1745, transported from Liverpool on the
Veteran bound for the Leeward Islands on 5 May 1747,
liberated and landed on Martinique in June 1747.
[NA.SP.36.102][JAB.2.431][P.2.306]

JOLLY, HENRY, a merchant in Bordeaux, 1677.
[NAS.GD164.1120]

JOSSY, HENRY, a merchant in Bordeaux, husband of Mary
Sinclair, an assignation, 1671, deeds, 1683, 1685.
[NAS.RD3.55.393; RD3.57.21; RD2.29.249;
RD2.66.114]

KARR, ANDREW SILVER, of Kippilaw, died in France on 22 July 1833, inventory, 1834, Comm. Edinburgh. [NAS]

KAY, THOMAS, a merchant in Antwerp, died 23 March 1841, inventory, 1843, Comm. Edinburgh. [NAS]

KEDSLIE, MARGARET, wife of John Gittens, died in Guadaloupe, 1853. [S.14.1854]

KEITH, GEORGE, born 12 September 1714, son of George Keith and his wife Isobel Leys, a shoemaker in Old Machar, Aberdeen, a Jacobite in 1745, transported from Liverpool on the <u>Veteran</u> bound for the Leeward Islands on 5 May 1747, liberated and landed on Martinique in June 1747. [NA.SP.36.102][JAB.2.432][P.2.308]

KELLO, PETER, from Edinburgh, graduated MD from Rheims University, 1681. [RCPE]

KEMP, ..., a Lieutenant of *Le Regiment Royal Ecossais*, 1754-1759. [JAHR]

KENNEDY, GILBERT, graduated MD from Rheims University, 1714. [RCPE]

KENNEDY, JAMES, a merchant in Calais, a letter,1685. [NAS.NRAS.464/19]

KENNEDY, JAMES, graduated MD from Rheims University, 1736. [RCPE]

KENNEDY, JAMES, born 1819, son of James Kennedy and his wife Mary Weir in Broughty Ferry, died in Port-au-Prince, 1844. [Dundee, Eastern Necropolis, MI]

KENNEDY, JAMESINA, in Nice, an inventory, 1875. [NAS.SC70.172/965]

KENNEDY, JOHN, born 1715, a laborer and a Jacobite from Perthshire, transported from Liverpool on the <u>Veteran</u> bound for the Leeward Islands on 5 May 1747, liberated and landed on Martinique in June 1747. [P.2.314][MR.154]

KENNEDY, MARY, born 1727, a washerwoman from Glengarry, a Jacobite in 1745, transported from Liverpool on the <u>Veteran</u> bound for the Leeward Islands on 5 May 1747, liberated and landed on Martinique in June 1747. [NA.SP.36.102][P.2.316]

KERR, ALEXANDER, a merchant in Bordeaux, 1763. [NAS.RS27.173.139]

KERR, DUGALD CAMPBELL, a merchant in Nantes, died 28 December 1858, inventory, 1859, Comm. Edinburgh. [NAS]

KERR, ROBERT, of Chatto, died in Nice on 6 December 1831, inventory, 1832, Comm. Edinburgh. [NAS]

KERR, ..., a Lieutenant of *Le Regiment Royal Ecossais*, 1748-1756. [JAHR]

KEYDEN, HELEN MORRISON, in Pau, heir to her mother Helen Grierson or Keyden in Helensburgh, Dunbartonshire, 25 September 1850. [NAS.S/H]

KILGOUR, ROBERT WILLIAM, of Tulloch, died in Trouville-sur-Mer on 13 July 1858, inventory, 1858, Comm. Edinburgh. [NAS]

KILPATRICK, THOMAS, a merchant in Bordeaux, was admitted as a burgess and guildsbrother of Ayr on 29 August 1688. [ABR]

KING, CLEMENT, a student at Montpellier University, 1600. [RCPE]

KING, GABRIEL, graduated MD from Rheims University, 1719. [RCPE]

KING, JOHN, from Aberdeen, a student at Montpellier University, and Orange University, 1630s. [RCPE]

KING, JOHN, died in Martinique during December 1787. Testament confirmed in Edinburgh on 28 December 1824. [NAS.CC8.8.150-1]

KING, ROBERT, MD, from Glasgow, died in Paris on 22 March 1829. [S#968]

KINKAID, ALEXANDER, a student at Montpellier University, 1611. [RCPE]

KINLOCH, FRANCIS, a merchant in Edinburgh and by 1661 in Paris, died before 1680, relict Margaret Aldison. [NAS.RD3.48.651; RD4.2.253; RD2.1.895; RD2.30.620; RD3.64.141; RD3.66.724]

KINLOCH, JOHN, graduated MD from Rheims University, 1712. [RCPE]

KINLOCH, KATHARINE, daughter of Jacob Kinloch of Stonyflat, and spouse of Alexander Gordon a factor in Bordeaux, a marriage contract, 1730. [NAS.RD3.210.46]

KINNINMONT, JOHN, born 1769, husband of Catherine Carstairs, died in France during 1815. [Kilconquhar, Fife, MI]

KIRKPATRICK, WILLIAM ESCOTT, in Brussels, heir to his aunt Jane Kirkpatrick in Nithbank, Dumfries, 23 September 1859. [NAS.S/H]

KNIE, BALTHASER, a weather-glass maker from France who settled in Edinburgh in 1794. [ECA.SL115.1.1]

KNIGHT, Captain HOOD, of the Royal Navy, died in Paris on 30 October 1823, inventory, 1836, Comm. Edinburgh. [NAS]

KYD, DAVID, born 1824, son of James Kyd, (1771-1848),a manufacturer in Barngreen, Arbroath, late of Dunkirk, France, died 25 July 1896, his wife Margaret Steven, born 1821, died in Landerneau, France, in 1857. [Arbroath Abbey MI]

LA CADET, PAUL, a perfumer from France who settled in
Edinburgh in 1781, residing in Liberton Wynd.
[ECA.SL115.1.1]

LACKY, JAMES, born 1731, a weaver in Edinburgh, a
Jacobite in 1745, transported from Liverpool on the
Veteran bound for the Leeward Islands on 5 May 1747,
liberated and landed on Martinique in June 1747.
[NA.SP.36.102][P.2.328]

LA HASSIE, PETER, a French dancing master in Edinburgh,
1704, 1705. [NAS.CH1.2.5.2.149; 175.1]

LA LAINE, PATRICK, a factor in Bordeaux, was admitted as
a burgess and guilds-brother of Ayr on 25 June 1687.
[ABR]

LAMB, JAMES, born 1722, a watchmaker in Edinburgh, a
Jacobite in 1745, transported from Liverpool on the
Veteran bound for the Leeward Islands on 5 May 1747,
liberated and landed on Martinique in June 1747.
[NA.SP.36.102][P.2.330]

LAUS, JAMES, a student at Caen University, 1687. [RCPE]

LA VIE, HENRI, a sailor from Bourdeaux, was admitted as a
burgess and guilds-brother of Ayr on 15 August 1660.
[ABR]; a merchant and factor in Bordeaux, deeds, 1671,
1672, 1680. [NAS.RD2.31.152/322/327;
RD2.32.190/300; RH15.106.387; SE#30]

LA VIE, HENRY, formerly in London, a merchant in
Bordeaux, deeds,1690, 1705. [NAS.RD3.73.116;
RD3.105.228, etc]

LA VIE, JOHN, son of Henry La Vie, a factor in Bordeaux,
was admitted as a burgess and guilds-brother of Ayr on
30 August 1686. [ABR]

LAW, JOHN, born in Edinburgh 21 April 1671, son of
William Law of Laurieston, a goldsmith in Edinburgh,
founder of the Mississippi Company of France,
(Compagnie de Indes), pre 1720. On 22 July 1719

Edinburgh Town Council admitted John Law, Lord and
Earl of Tankerville in France, Director General of the
Royal Bank and Indian Company of France, as a burgess
and guildsbrother of Edinburgh by right of his father
John Law of Lauriston a burgess and guilds-brother. He
died in Venice on 21 March 1729. [NAS.GD44/43/9;
GD45.16.3013] [Roll of Edinburgh Burgessses]

LAW, WILLIAM, in Paris, 1765. [NAS.RD2.197.930/939]

LAWRENTINE, ROGER, a factor in Bordeaux, 1628.
[NAS.AC7.1.153]

LAWRIE, PETER, a merchant in Guadaloupe before 1782.
[NAS.CS17.1.1]

LAWSON, JAMES, born 1725, a workman in Wester Coull,
Lintrathen, Angus, a Jacobite soldier of Ogilvy's
Regiment in 1745, imprisoned at Carlisle, transported
from Liverpool on the _Veteran_ bound for the Leeward
Islands on 5 May 1747, liberated and landed on
Martinique in June 1747.
[P.2.234][OR34][NA.SP.36.102][LPR.220]

LAWSON, MARGARET, born 1852 in Landemieau, France,
daughter of James Lawson, buried in Dundee on 15
September 1854. [Dundee burial register]

LEARMONT, JOHN, graduated MD from Rheims University
in 1719. [NAS.NRAS.726.3.36]

LEARMONT, WILLIAM, graduated MD from Rheims
University, 1700. [RCPE][NAS.NRAS.726.3.11]

LE FORT, or CORUILLE, LOUIS, a periwig maker in
Canongate, Edinburgh, bonds, 1680. [NAS.RD4.46.577;
RD4.47.51]

LE GENDRE, JULES, born in Chartres, France, on 28
February 1785, a Lieutenant of the Imperial French
Guards, died in Dundee on 1 September 1840, husband
of Jane Inches born in Dunkeld on 29 July 1780, died in
Glasgow on 23 December 1848, parents of Jules and

William Cheviller Le Gendre (who was buried in Dundee 23 May 1824). [Dundee, Howff, gravestone] [Dundee burial register]

LEITH, JOHN, an Ensign of *Le Regiment d'Ogilvie*, 1760. [JAHR]

LE LEYER, PHILBERT, a merchant in Landemain, 1725. [NAS.AC9.888]

LERMONT, JOHN, graduated MD from Rheims University, 1680. [RCPE]

LESLIE, Sir JAMES, of Pitcaple, a Major General of the French Army, died in Thionville, Luxembourg on 24 May 1757. [Aberdeen Journal Obituaries]

LESLIE, PATRICK, graduated MD from Rheims University, 1726. [RCPE]

LETHAM, WILLIAM, was admitted as a burgess and guilds-brother of Glasgow on 27 September 1627 as he was bound as an army officer to aid in the relief of La Rochelle. [GBR]

LETUS, JAMES, from Aberdeen, a student at Paris University, 1603. [RCPE]

LEWIS, Miss MAGDALENE, died at Pechbonieu near Toulouse on 23 March 1829, inventory, 1829, Comm. Edinburgh. [NAS]

LIDDERDALE, THOMAS, from Edinburgh, graduated MD from Rheims University, 1729. [RCPE]

LIGORIE, JAMES, a factor in Le Croisic, 1628. [NAS.AC7.1.153]

LIND, FRANCIS, graduated MD from Rheims University, 1727. [RCPE]

LINDSAY, ROBERT, possibly from Jedburgh, graduated MD from Rheims University, 1749. [RCPE]

LITTLE, EDWARD, a merchant in Paris, son of the late
William Little merchant and provost of Edinburgh, 1612,
1613. [NAS.GD122.2.965; GD122.15.11]

LITTLEJOHN, JAMES, son of Peter Littlejohn in the Mains
of Hazlehead, Aberdeen, died in Guadaloupe, 1760.
[ACA. APB.2.215]

LIVINGSTON, ..., a Captain of *Le Regiment d'Ogilvie*,
1748-1757. [JAHR]

LOCKHART, GRACE, widow of Colonel Lewis Mackenzie,
eldest son of Sir Roderick Mackenzie of Scatwell, died
in Dunkirk on 26 August 1848. [EEC#21705]

LOCKHART, Colonel WILLIAM, Governor of Dunkirk,
1660s. [NAS.NRAS.332/F2/231, 330]

LOISEREL, JEAN, a French soldier, captured in the West
Indies aboard the Mary Ann, a prisoner of war in
Greenlaw, Scotland, died there16 March 1809.
[NA.ADM1903/155/102; 103/624, 648]

LOWIS, ROBERT, graduated MD from Rheims University,
1706. [NAS.NRAS.726.3.18]

LOWNDES, JOHN, formerly of Arthurley, Renfrewshire,
died at his residence in Rue d'Agusseau, Paris, on 21
December 1840, aged 74. [W#II/104]

LUCAS, JOHN, a student at Montpellier University, 1607.
[RCPE]

LUMSDEN, JAMES, graduated MD from Rheims University,
1681. [RCPE]

LUMSDEN, THOMAS, a Master of Arts, Paris, a deed, 1669.
[NAS.RD2.26.87]

LUNDIN, ..., a Lieutenant of *Le Regiment Royal Ecossais*,
1745-1761. [JAHR]

LUSSIGNET, JOHN, a merchant in Bordeaux, deeds, 1670, 1673, 1687,1690. [NAS.RD3.23.281; RD4.33.551; RD3.66.64; RD4.65.20]

LUTFUTT, JAMES, from Edinburgh, a student at Orange University, 1700. [RCPE]

LYON, CHARLES, a Captain of *Le Regiment d'Ogilvie,* 1760. [JAHR]

LYONS, MATTHIAS, a Writer to the Signet, died in Paris on 3 June 1836, inventory, 1837, Comm. Edinburgh. [NAS]

MCADAM, WILLIAM, a merchant and servant of Daniel Mason a merchant in St Martins, France, a deed of factory, 1680. [NAS.RD2.52.525]

MCALEXANDER, ANDREW, a merchant in Bordeaux, around 1640. [NAS.GD18/2361; SE#29]

MACBEAN, DONALD, a Lieutenant of *Le Regiment Royal Ecossais,* 1749-1769. [JAHR]

MACBEAN, WILLIAM, from Inverness, Lieutenant of the Triton of Nantes, who died in 1828. [NAS.GD23/6/647]

MACCALESTER, JACK, aged 32, his wife aged 25, and their children Elisabeth aged 9, and Jack aged 5, settled in Louisiana in 1797. [NWI.II.229]

MCCORMACK, MARK, born 1731, a laborer in Moidart, Inverness-shire, a Jacobite in 1745, transported from Liverpool on the Veteran bound for the Leeward Islands on 5 May 1747, liberated and landed on Martinique in June 1747. [NA.SP.36.102][P.3.28]

MCCREDIE, WILLIAM, from Ayr, graduated MD from Rheims University, 1753. [RCPE]

MCCULLOCH, JAMES, born 1750, son of William McCulloch and Joanna Runcie, a student at the Scots College at Douai, 1763. [RSC.I.92]

MCCULLOCH, ROBERT, from Tain, graduated MD from Rheims University, 1680. [RCPE]

MCDANIEL, DANIEL, born in France, master of the Dolphin seized by the British at Montserrat, 1736. [SPAWI.1737.93xi]

MACDONALD, AENEAS, a factor in Paris, 1741. [NAS.AC10.284]

MACDONALD, ALEXANDER, a Lieutenant of *Le Regiment Royal Ecossais*, 1756-1761. [JAHR]

MCDONALD, DANIEL, born 1728, a laborer in Lettochbeag, Kinloch, Inverness-shire, a Jacobite in 1745, transported from Liverpool on the Veteran bound for the Leeward Islands on 5 May 1747, liberated and landed on Martinique in June 1747. [NA.SP.36.102][P.3.52]

MCDONALD, DANIEL, aged 22, born in Scotland, a Sergeant of *Le Regiment d'Ogilvie*, 17... [JAHR]

MCDONALD, DONALD, born 1689, a servant in Edinburgh, a Jacobite in 1745, transported from Liverpool on the Veteran bound for the Leeward Islands on 5 May 1747, liberated and landed on Martinique in June 1747. [NA.SP.36.102]

MCDONALD, DONALD, born 1725, a laborer in Inverness, a Jacobite in 1745, transported from Liverpool on the Veteran bound for the Leeward Islands on 5 May 1747, liberated and landed on Martinique in June 1747. [NA.SP.36.102][P.3.56]

MCDONALD, DONALD, Captain of Lord Lewis Drummond's French Regiment, a deed, 8 March 1750. [NAS.RD4.177/1.201]

MCDONALD, GEORGE, aged 23, born in Reay, Scotland, a Corporal of *Le Regiment d'Ogilvie*, 17... [JAHR]

MCDONALD, HUGH, born 1734, from Arisaig, Inverness-shire, a Jacobite in 1745, transported from Liverpool on

the Veteran bound for the Leeward Islands on 5 May
1747, liberated and landed on Martinique in June 1747.
[NA.SP.36.102][P.3.62]

MCDONALD, JOHN, a Captain of *Le Regiment d'Ogilvie,*
1747. [JAHR]

MCDONALD, JOSEPH, born 1720, a weaver in Morayshire,
a Jacobite in 1745, transported from Liverpool on the
Veteran bound for the Leeward Islands on 5 May 1747,
liberated and landed on Martinique in June 1747.
[NA.SP.36.102][P.3.72]

MCDONALD, MARGARET, born 1724, a spinner in
Perthshire, a Jacobite in 1745, transported from
Liverpool on the Veteran bound for the Leeward Islands
on 5 May 1747, liberated and landed on Martinique in
June 1747. [NA.SP.36.102]

MCDONALD, RONALD, a Captain of *Le Regiment Royal
Ecossais,* 1745-1761. [JAHR]

MACDONELL OF GLENGARRY, ALEXANDER ROY,
an officer of *Le Regiment Royal Ecossais,* 1744, captured
at sea by the Royal Navy and imprisoned in the Tower of
London in 1746. [JAHR]

MACDONELL, ALLAN, a Captain of *Le Regiment d'Ogilvie,*
1747-1756. [JAHR]

MACDONELL, ALLAN, born in Argyll, Scotland, a soldier
of *Le Regiment d'Ogilvie,* 1762. [JAHR]

MACDONELL, ANGUS, a Lieutenant of *Le Regiment
d'Ogilvy,* 1760. [JAHR]

MACDONELL, ARCHIBALD, a Lieutenant of *Le Regiment
d'Ogilvie,* 1746-1760. [JAHR]

MACDONELL, CHARLES, an Ensign of *Le Regiment
d'Ogilvie,* 1760. [JAHR]

MACDONELL, DONALD, of LOCH GARRY, a Captain of
Le Regiment d'Ogilvie, 1747. [JAHR]

MACDONELL, JAMES, a Captain of *le Regiment d'Albanie*, 1748. [JAHR]
MACDONELL, JOHN, a Lieutenant of Grenadiers in *Le Regiment d'Ogilvy*, 1757. [JAHR]

MACDONELL, RANALD, a Lieutenant of the Grenadiers in *Le Regiment d'Ogilvie*, 1759. [JAHR]

MACDONELL, NEIL, a Lieutenant of Grenadiers in *Le Regiment d'Ogilvy*, 1747. [JAHR]

MACDONELL of CLANRANALD, ..., an officer of *Le Regiment Royal Ecossais*, 1744. [JAHR]

MCDOUGALL, ALLAN, born 1721, a gardener in Strathlachlan, Argyll, a Jacobite in 1745, transported from Liverpool on the Veteran bound for the Leeward Islands on 5 May 1747, liberated and landed on Martinique in June 1747. [NA.SP.36.102][P.3.80]

MCDOWAL, ROBERT, from Edinburgh, graduated MD from Rheims University, 1747. [RCPE]

MCEWEN, JOHN, in Martinique, testament, 21 April 1813, Comm. Edinburgh. [NAS.CC8.8.139.84]

MCFARLANE, ELIZABETH, born 1717, a sewer in Perth, a Jacobite in 1745, transported from Liverpool on the Veteran bound for the Leeward Islands on 5 May 1747, liberated and landed on Martinique in June 1747. [NA.SP.36.102][P.3.88]

MCFARLANE, WILLIAM, graduated MD from Rheims University, 1725; 1727. [RCPE][NAS.NRAS.726.3.53]

MCFARQUHAR, Miss MARGARET, in Manchester, died in France, 29 May 1856, inventory, 1856, Comm. Edinburgh. [NAS]

MCFEE, HUGH, born 1717, a laborer in Inverness, a Jacobite in 1745, transported from Liverpool on the Veteran bound for the Leeward Islands on 5 May 1747, liberated

and landed on Martinique in June 1747.
[NA.SP.36.102][P.3.172]

MCGHIE, JOHN, from Edinburgh, graduated MD from
Rheims University, 1686. [RCPE]

MCGILLIES, DANIEL, born 1735, a laborer in Arisaig,
Inverness-shire, a Jacobite in 1745, transported from
Liverpool on the Veteran bound for the Leeward Islands
on 5 May 1747, liberated and landed on Martinique in
June 1747. [NA.SP.36.102][P.3.90]

MCGILLIS, DONALD, born 1729, a laborer in Inverness, a
Jacobite in 1745, transported from Liverpool on the
Veteran bound for the Leeward Islands on 5 May 1747,
liberated and landed on Martinique in June 1747.
[NA.SP.36.102][P.3.90]

MCGILLIS, HECTOR, born 1731, a herd in Inverness, a
Jacobite in 1745, transported from Liverpool on the
Veteran bound for the Leeward Islands on 5 May 1747,
liberated and landed on Martinique in June 1747.
[NA.SP.36.102][P.3.90]

MCGILVARY, ..., Lieutenant of the 1st [Royal Scots]
Regiment, died in St Domingo, 1796.
[NAS.GD188.28.6]

MCGRANE, MICHAEL, in Bordeaux, a burgess of Arbroath,
1791. [Arbroath Burgess Roll: Angus Archives, #18/941]
[NAS.CE70.1.7]

MCGRATH, NICOLAS, an officer of *Le Regiment Royal
Ecossais*, 1744. [JAHR]

MCGREGOR, HUGH, born 1803, a bleaching master,
formerly of Claverhouse, Dundee, died in Pont de
Nieppe, Department du Nord, France, on 17 July 1866.
[DA#1641]

MCGREGOR, Sir WILLIAM, of Balhadies, a Jacobite who
fled to France in 1716, died in Paris during 1765.
[JP#97]

MCGREGOR, ALEXANDER, from Touhos near Stirling, a soldier of the Grenadier Company of *Le Regiment d'Albanie*, 1748. [JAHR]

MCGREGOR, ..., a Lieutenant of *Le Regiment Royal Ecossais*, 1745-1759. [JAHR]

MCGRIGOR of GLENGYLE,......, an officer of *Le Regiment Royal Ecossais*, 1744. [JAHR]

MACGUIDOEM (?), JAMES, from Perth, graduated MD from Rheims University, 1772. [RCPE]

MCHARDY, JOHN, a soldier of the Grenadier Company of *Le Regiment d'Albanie*, 1748. [JAHR]

MCINTOSH, ANGUS, born 1721, a laborer in Inverness-shire, a Jacobite in 1745, transported from Liverpool on the Veteran bound for the Leeward Islands on 5 May 1747, liberated and landed on Martinique in June 1747. [NA.SP.36.102][P.3.100]

MACINTOSH, ANGUS, born in Inverness, Scotland, a soldier of *Le Regiment d'Ogilvie*, 1762. [JAHR]

MCINTOSH, DUNCAN, a Captain of *Le Regiment d'Ogilvie*, 1747. [JAHR]

MCINTOSH, DUNCAN, settled in Dominica during 1761, land grant in St Anne's parish in 1765, moved to St Pierre, Martinique, in July 1774. [NAS.NRAS.771/306; GD126, box 4]

MCINTOSH, JANE, born 1727, a knitter in Inverness, a Jacobite in 1745, transported from Liverpool on the Veteran bound for the Leeward Islands on 5 May 1747, liberated and landed on Martinique in June 1747. [NA.SP.36.102][P.3.102]

MCINTOSH, JOHN, born 1696, a fiddler in Inverness, a Jacobite in 1745, transported from Liverpool on the Veteran bound for the Leeward Islands on 5 May 1747,

liberated and landed on Martinique in June 1747.
[NA.SP.36.102][P.3.102]

MACINTOSH, JOHN, born in Inverness, Scotland, a soldier
of *Le Regiment d'Ogilvie,* 1762. [JAHR]

MCINTOSH, LACHLAN, a Captain of Grenadiers in *Le
Regiment d'Ogilvie,* 1747. [JAHR]

MCINTOSH, PETER, born 1713, a laborer in Inverness, a
Jacobite in 1745, transported from Liverpool on the
Veteran bound for the Leeward Islands on 5 May 1747,
liberated and landed on Martinique in June 1747.
[NA.SP.36.102][P.3.102]

MCINTOSH of STRATHARN, ..., Captain of *Le Regiment
d'Ogilvie,* 1747. [JAHR]

MCINTOSH, Miss, youngest daughter of William McIntosh
in Grenada, married Chevalier le Sieur de Colleville, in
Ostend, 1791. [GM.61.1061]

MCINTOSH, ..., surgeon, died in St Domingo, 1796.
[NAS.GD188.28.6]

MCKAIL, MATTHEW, from Aberdeen, graduated MD from
Rheims University, 1713. [RCPE]

MCKAY, ALEXANDER, a mill overseer in Landerneau,
Brest, died on 28 February 1851, inventory, 1851,
Commissariat of Edinburgh. [NAS]

MACKENE, DAVID, in Rouen 1643. [NAS.GD18.2431]

MCKENZIE, ALEXANDER, from Elgin, graduated MD
from Rheims University, 1739. [RCPE]

MCKENZIE, GEORGE, graduated MD from Rheims
University, 1733. [RCPE]

MCKENZIE, HENRY PATRICK JOHNSTONE, in St
Malo, an inventory, 1873. [NAS.SC70.179.375]

MCKENZIE, JANE, born 1728, a sewer in Inverness, a Jacobite in 1745, transported from Liverpool on the Veteran bound for the Leeward Islands on 5 May 1747, liberated and landed on Martinique in June 1747. [NA.SP.36.102][P.3.124]

MCKENZIE, JOHN, born 1715, a gentleman in Ardloch, Assynt, Sutherland, a Jacobite in 1745, transported from Liverpool on the Veteran bound for the Leeward Islands on 5 May 1747, liberated and landed on Martinique in June 1747. [NA.SP.36.102][P.3.124]

MCKENZIE, JOHN, in Menton, France, administration, 14 March 1883. [NAS.SC70/6]

MCKENZIE, MARY, born 1727, a spinner in Lochaber, Inverness-shire, a Jacobite in 1745, transported from Liverpool on the Veteran bound for the Leeward Islands on 5 May 1747, liberated and landed on Martinique in June 1747. [NA.SP.36.102][P.3.130]

MCKENZIE, MURDOCH, graduated MD from Rheims University, 1728. [RCPE]

MACKENZIE, R., an officer of *Le Regiment Royal Ecossais*, 1744. [JAHR]

MACKENZIE, WILLIAM, Marquis of Seaforth, son of Kenneth Mackenzie and his wife Frances Herbert, a Jacobite who fought at Sheriffmuir in 1715, fled to France, died on the isle of Lewis on 8 January 1740. [JP#163][SP.VII.511]

MCKENZIE, WILLIAM, from Ross-shire, graduated MD from Rheims University, 1739. [RCPE]

MCKERCHER,......, a Scot, in Maryland 1737 as agent for the French tobacco company. [SPAWI.1737.467]

MACKERRALL, ROBERT, a merchant and factor in La Rochelle, was admitted as a burgess and guilds-brother of Ayr in 1690. [ABR]

MACKIE, DANIEL, born 1729, a labourer in Morayshire, a Jacobite in 1745, transported from Liverpool on the Veteran bound for the Leeward Islands on 5 May 1747, liberated and landed on Martinique in June 1747. [NA.SP.36.102][P.3.108]

MCLANE, ..., medical storekeeper, died in St Domingo, 1796. [NAS.GD188.28.6]

MACLAY, KENNETH, in Martinique, 1799. [SA#260]

MCLEAN, JAMES, born 1728, a nail-maker in Stirling, a Jacobite in 1745, transported from Liverpool on the Veteran bound for the Leeward Islands on 5 May 1747, liberated and landed on Martinique in June 1747. [NA.SP.36.102][P.3.148]

MCLEAN, WILLIAM, born 1715, a laborer in Inverness, a Jacobite in 1745, transported from Liverpool on the Veteran bound for the Leeward Islands on 5 May 1747, liberated and landed on Martinique in June 1747. [NA.SP.36.102][P.3.152]

MCLEISH, DUNCAN, born 1729, a pedlar in Perthshire, a Jacobite in 1745, transported from Liverpool on the Veteran bound for the Leeward Islands on 5 May 1747, liberated and landed on Martinique in June 1747. [NA.SP.36.102][P.3.152]

MCLEOD, ALEXANDER, born 1728, a labourer in Perthshire, a Jacobite in 1745, transported from Liverpool on the Veteran bound for the Leeward Islands on 5 May 1747, liberated and landed on Martinique in June 1747. [NA.SP.36.102][P.3.156]

MCLEOD, JOHN, born 1722, a laborer, a Jacobite in 1745, transported from Liverpool on the Veteran bound for the Leeward Islands on 5 May 1747, liberated and landed on Martinique in June 1747. [NA.SP.36.102][P.3.162]

MCLEOD, KATHERINE, youngest daughter of Alexander Norman McLeod of Harris, married M. de Bourboulon the French minister to China, in Baltimore on 28 April 1851. [W#1234]

MCMATH, HECTOR, in Rouen and Dieppe, 1635-1637. [NAS.GD18.2366]

MCMATH, NICHOLAS, a factor in Dieppe, pre-1644. [SE#28][RGS.XI.581]

MACNAB, ..., Ensign of *Le Regiment Royal Ecossais*, 1757-1761. [JAHR]

MCNEAL, HECTOR, born in Rosebank, Roslin, on 22 October 1746, later in Guadaloupe. [NAS.NRAS.0052]

MCPHERSON, ARCHIBALD, born 1731, a cowherd in the Isle of Skye, a Jacobite in 1745, transported from Liverpool on the Veteran bound for the Leeward Islands on 5 May 1747, liberated and landed on Martinique in June 1747. [NA.SP.36.102][P.3.176]

MCPHERSON, DUNCAN, a Jacobite in 1745, transported from Liverpool on the Veteran bound for the Leeward Islands on 5 May 1747, liberated and landed on Martinique in June 1747. [NA.SP.36.102][P.3.176]

MACPHERSON, or GAUTRET, EUDORA, in France, heir to her uncle Duncan MacPherson, a Lieutenant of the 52nd Regiment of Foot, who died 15 March 1855. [NAS.S/H]

MCPHERSON, JAMES, born 1725, a laborer in Aberdeen, a Jacobite in 1745, transported from Liverpool on the Veteran bound for the Leeward Islands on 5 May 1747, liberated and landed on Martinique in June 1747. [NA.SP.36.102][P.3.176]

MACPHERSON, JOHN, in Martinique, 1799. [SA#260]

MCPHERSON, WILLIAM, in Martinique, letters, 1800. [NAS.NRAS.771/985]

MCPHERSON, ..., an officer of *Le Regiment Royal Ecossais*, 1744. [JAHR]

MAITLAND, WILLIAM, graduated MD from Rheims University, 1717. [RCPE]

MALCOLM, CHARLES, from Fife, graduated MD from Rheims University, 1681. [RCPE]

MANLY, THOMAS, a student at Montpellier University, 1611. [RCPE]

MANN, JAMES, born 1727, a baker in Dunkeld, Perthshire, a Jacobite in 1745, transported from Liverpool on the Veteran bound for the Leeward Islands on 5 May 1747, liberated and landed on Martinique in June 1747. [NA.SP.36.102][P.3.6]

MANSION, GEORGE LOUIS HORACE, born 17 October 1873 in Dreux, France, died in St John Dalry, Kirkcudbrightshire, on 15 November 1888. [Dalry gravestone]

MARGOLIE, JOHN, Commander of a French privateer, 26 June 1797. [NAS.CE70.1.8]

MARJORIBANKS, EDWARD, in Montpellier, France, a deed of factory and commission, 26 February 1752. [NAS.RD3.211/2.137]

MARNOCH, ALEXANDER, born 1 May 1720, a shoemaker in St Nicholas, Aberdeen, a Jacobite in 1745, transported from Liverpool on the Veteran bound for the Leeward Islands on 5 May 1747, liberated and landed on Martinique in June 1747. [NA.SP.36.102][JAB.2.436]

MARSHALL, JAMES, a tailor in Paris, a deed of factory, 1682. [NAS.RD3.51.292]

MARTIN, ABRAHAM, known as "l'Ecossais', born 1589 in France, settled in New France around 1620, a pilot, died in Quebec during 1664. [DCB.I.495]

MARTINE, ABRAHAM, born in 1616, son of Abraham
Martine a merchant burgess of Metz, Lorraine, settled in
Dundee, Scotland, as a surgeon barber, died on 13 June
1673, husband of Sarah Auchenleck, born 1625, died on
25 July 1665. [Dundee MI]

MARTINE, ALEXANDER, a student at Cahors University,
1631. [RCPE]

MARTIN, MARTIN, graduated MD from Rheims University,
1716. [RCPE]

MASON, JOHN, born 29 June 1727, son of William Mason
and his wife Helen Mouat in Old Machar,
Aberdeenshire, a barber in Aberdeen, a Jacobite in 1745,
transported from Liverpool on the Veteran bound for the
Leeward Islands on 5 May 1747, liberated and landed on
Martinique in June 1747. [NA.SP.36.102][JAB.2.436]

MASSON, ADAM, a merchant in La Rochelle, a bond, 15
November 1661. [NAS.RD4.3.674]

MASSOUN, DANIEL, son of Daniel Massoun, a factor and
merchant in La Rochelle, a deed of factory, 1680; was
admitted as a burgess and guilds-brother of Ayr on 18
June 1698. [NAS.RD2.52.525][ABR]

MATTHEW, ANDREW, born 1715, a maltster in Perthshire,
a Jacobite in 1745, transported from Liverpool on the
Veteran bound for the Leeward Islands on 5 May 1747,
liberated and landed on Martinique in June 1747.
[NA.SP.36.102][P.3.12]

MATTHEWSON, Lieutenant P., in Guadaloupe, 1811.
[NAS.GD327.510]

MAULE, JAMES, Earl of Panmure, son of George Maule, a
Jacobite who fought at Sheriffmuir in 1715, fled to
France, died in Paris on 23 April 1723, at La Ville
d'Hambourg, Ruse des Boucheries, Faubourg Saint
Germain, parish of St Sulpice.
[SP.VII.26][CRA.233][NAS.E650.79]

Scots-French Links in Europe and America, 1550-1850

MAXWELL, Major BRYCE, son of Provost Edward Maxwell and his wife Charlotte Blair, died in Martinique during 1809. [St Michael's, Dumfries, MI]

MAXWELL, Miss GEORGINA GORDON, in Paris, died at Versailles on 26 March 1858, inventory, 1858, Comm. Edinburgh. [NAS]

MAXWELL, JANE ELIZABETH NORAH, in Paris, died 15 March 1846, inventory, 1847, Comm. Edinburgh. [NAS]

MAXWELL, THOMAS, a captain in the Earl of Dunbarton's Regiment in France, a bond, 1676. [NAS.RD2.41.165]

MAXWELL, WALTER, Captain of a Scots Regiment in France, husband of Janet Maxwell, a bond, 1678. [NAS.RD4.42.323]

MAXWELL, ..., Ensign of *Le Regiment Royal Ecossais*, 1753-1759. [JAHR]

MEASON, or BENGNOT, or WEMYSS, Madame MARY JOSEPHINE, in Paris, died 17 May 1858, inventory, 1858, Comm. Edinburgh. [NAS]

MEL, MICHEL, a merchant in Dieppe, 1650s. [NAS.GD18.2371]

MELL, WILLIAM, in Rouen, a deed, 1696; in Edinburgh, formerly a merchant in France, deeds, 1700, 1707. [NAS.RD4.78.528; RD4.87.662/670; RD4.100.1184]

MELVEN, JAMES, of HM Guard in France, 1612. [NAS.GD122.2.965]

MENZIES, JEANNIE NEWBIGGING, born in Hoddam on 23 September 1845, daughter of Reverend Robert Menzies and his wife Martha Coldstream, died in Hyeres, France, on 8 March 1892. [F.2.249]

MENZIES, WALTER, born 1729, a flaxdresser in Atholl, Perthshire, a Jacobite in 1745, transported from Liverpool on the <u>Veteran</u> bound for the Leeward Islands on 5 May 1747, liberated and landed on Martinique in June 1747. [NA.SP.36.102][P.3.188]

MENZIES, ..., a Lieutenant of *Le Regiment Royal Ecossais*, 1745-1759. [JAHR]

MERCER, JOHN, a factor in Bordeaux, a deed, 1707. [NAS.RD4.100.568; CS96/3309]

MESTON, Reverend WILLIAM, in Lille, heir to his brother Thomas Meston a teacher in Aberdeen who died on 28 April 1851, 16 June 1852. [NAS.S/H]

MIDDLETON, ALEXANDER, born 1706, a servant in Edinburgh or Aberdeen, a Jacobite in 1745, transported from Liverpool on the Veteran bound for the Leeward Islands on 5 May 1747, liberated and landed on Martinique in June 1747. [NA.SP.36.102][P.3.190]

MIKARTI, MARIE, born 25 August 1714, daughter of .....Mikarti, an English sergeant, and his wife Isabelle Bole, and baptised on 11 March 1716 in the Church of St Jean Baptiste, Annapolis Royal, Acadia. [NSARM.RG1, Vol.26/139]

MILL, ANDREW, born 1730, a tailor in Banffshire, a Jacobite in 1745, transported from Liverpool on the Veteran bound for the Leeward Islands on 5 May 1747, liberated and landed on Martinique in June 1747. [NA.SP.36.102] [JAB.2.437][P.2.196]

MILLER, JOHN, from Edinburgh, a student at Caen University, 1669. [RCPE]

MILLS, WILLIAM, born 1725, a servant in Aberdeen, a Jacobite in 1745, transported from Liverpool on the Veteran bound for the Leeward Islands on 5 May 1747, liberated and landed on Martinique in June 1747. [NA.SP.36.102][P.2.196]

MIRASSON, JOSEPH, born 1814 in France, a French teacher in Edinburgh by 1851. [Census]

MITCHELL, DAVID, from Edinburgh, graduated MD from Rheims University, 1686. [RCPE]

MITCHELL, JOHN, graduated MD from Rheims University, 1713. [RCPE]

MITCHELL, ROBERT, graduated MD from Rheims University, 1720. [RCPE]

MOINET, VINCENT, valet to Mr Murray of Simprin at Baxter's Buildings, Leith Walk, Edinburgh, in 1794. [ECA.SL115.1.1]

MOIR, JOHN, son of Alexander Moir and his wife Janet Clerk in Fintry, Aberdeenshire, settled in France, 1586. [MSC.II.23]

MOIR, JOHN, born 1810 in France, a physician in Edinburgh by 1851. [Census]

MONCRIEFF, ELIZABETH, wife of Thomas Brown in France formerly in Crail, Fife, 1672. [NAS.RD4.31.320]

MONCRIEFF, JOHN, graduated MD from Rheims University, 1723. [RCPE]

MONRO, ALEXANDER, Lieutenant Colonel of the Earl of Dunbarton's regiment in France, bonds, 1676. [NAS,RD4.30.796, etc]

MONRO, DAVID, of Culcairn, died in Boulogne-sur-Mer on 17 March 1821. [S.5.219]

MONRO, DUNCAN, born 1728, a laborer in Inverness, a Jacobite in 1745, transported from Liverpool on the Veteran bound for the Leeward Islands on 5 May 1747, liberated and landed on Martinique in June 1747. [NA.SP.36.102][P.3.204]

MONTGOMERIE, NICHOLAS, graduated MD from Rheims University in 1709. [NAS.NRAS.726.3.22]

MORAY, JOHN, son of Moray of Abercairney, a Lieutenant Colonel of the French Army from 1693 to 1701. [NAS.GD24.1.368]

MORGAN, CHARLES, born 1729, a barber in Elgin, Morayshire, a Jacobite in 1745, transported from Liverpool on the Veteran bound for the Leeward Islands on 5 May 1747, liberated and landed on Martinique in June 1747. [NA.SP.36.102][P.3.208]

MORGAN, ..., Lieutenant of the 1st [Royal Scots] Regiment, died in St Domingo, 1796. [NAS.GD188.28.6]

MORISON, ALEXANDER, a student at Montpellier University, 1600. [RCPE]

MORISON, JAMES, born 1768, son of Alexander Morison of Bogrie, died in Paris on 3 May 1840. [AJ#4819]

MORISON, Colonel JAMES, in Boulogne sur Mer, died 30 May 1865, inventory, 1865, Comm. Edinburgh. [NAS]

MORISON, ROBERT, at Angers University, 1648. [RCPE]

MORLET, NICHOLAS, a merchant in Rouen, 1678. [NAS.AC7.4]

MORRIS, ANDREW, graduated MD from Rheims University, 1736. [RCPE]

MORRISON, GEORGE, Customs Collector at Fort Royal and at Trinite, Martinique, 1809. [NAS.NRAS.3585/4/6/12]

MOUNSEY, JAMES, graduated MD from Rheims University, 1739. [RCPE]

MOWAT, JAMES, a tailor in Paris 1640s. [NAS.GD18.2371]

MOWAT, JAMES, a merchant and banker in Paris, tailor to the Queen of France, in Edinburgh by 1674, deeds, 1666, 1669, 1670,1673, 1675, 1678, 1679. [NAS.RD4.34.549; RD3.37.365; RD4.25.724/756; RD4.26.159/181;

RD4.33.107/185/309; RD4.15.881; RD2.16.734;
RD2.17.109; RD2.26.87/175/382; RD2.38.541;
RD4.23.357; RD4.42.67; RD4.45.419]
[NAS.GD122.2.597]

MOWBRAY, FRANCIS, an archer of the Scots Guards of
France, 1560s. [NAS.NRAS.0.143]

MOYSANT, STEPHEN, a merchant in Rouen and a burgess
of Edinburgh, deed, 1670. [NAS.RD2.28.704]

MUDIE, JOHN, graduated MD from Rheims University,
1753. [RCPE]

MUIR, ANDREW P., a merchant from Glasgow, died in
Marseilles on 28 September 1831. [S.15.1230]

MUIR, WILLIAM, an officer of *Le Regiment Royal Ecossais,*
1744. [JAHR]

MUIRHEAD, JAMES, a burgess of Rouen (?), a deed, 1685.
[NAS.RD4.57.485]

MULART, JOSEPH, born in Quisnefage, France, a soldier of
the 26th Regiment, captured on Martinique, a prisoner of
war in Edinburgh Castle, died 28 December 1813, buried
at Greyfriars. [NA.ADM.103.114/1365, 103.648]

MUNRO, ALEXANDER, a Lieutenant Colonel of Lord
Douglas's Regiment 1670; Lieutenant Colonel of the
Earl of Dunfermline's Regiment in France, 1676;
Captain of Lord George Douglas's Regiment in France,
1681. [NAS.RD4.26.503; RD4.39.199; RD2.54.535]

MUNRO, ROBERT, born 1864, son of William Munro a
slater in Broughton Street, Edinburgh, died in
Guadaloupe on 26 March 1885. [S#13030]

MUNRO, ..., hospital purveyor, died in St Domingo, 1796.
[NAS.GD188.28.6]

MURRAY, GEORGE, graduated MD from Rheims
University, 1712. [RCPE]

MURRAY, GEORGE, from Stirling, graduated MD from Rheims University, 1717. [RCPE]

MURRAY, JAMES, born 1690 son of David Murray, Viscount Stormont, and his wife Marjory Scott, a Jacobite in 1715, died in Avignon, France, in August 1770. [JP.44][SP.VIII.205]

MURRAY, JOHN, born 1717, a weaver in Annandale, Dumfries-shire, a Jacobite in 1745, transported from Liverpool on the <u>Veteran</u> bound for the Leeward Islands on 5 May 1747, liberated and landed on Martinique in June 1747. [NA.SP.36.102][MR#124]

MURRAY, JOHN, Deputy Commissary General in St Domingo, 1796. [NAS.GD188.28.6]

MURRAY, or IRONSIDE, Mrs MARIANNE LLOYD, died in France, 16 July 1862, inventory, 1863, Comm. Edinburgh. [NAS]

NAGLE, or TELFER, JANE, wife of Patrick Nagle, in Maquetra, Boulogne sur Mer, died 17 February 1850, inventory, 1850, [Comm. Edinburgh. [NAS]

NAIRN, DAVID, second son of Sir John Nairn of Sanfurd, now in France, 2 March 1687. [NAS.Lyon Office, 10-2, 14-130]

NAIRN, HENRY, a Captain of *Le Regiment Royal Ecossais*, 1745. [JAHR]

NAIRN, JOHN, an officer of *Le Regiment Royal Ecossais*, 1744. [JAHR]

NAIRN, THOMAS, a Captain of *Le Regiment Royal Ecossais*, 1745-1747; and a Captain of *Le Regiment d'Albanie*, 1748. [JAHR]

NAPIER, JOHN, graduated MD from Rheims University, 1735. [RCPE]

NASMYTH, JOHN, surgeon to the King of France, and to the Scots Guards of France, died in London on 16 September 1613. [Edinburgh, Greyfriars, MI]

NASMITH, JAMES, from Edinburgh, graduated MD from Rheims University, 1749. [RCPE]

NEILSON, JAMES, born 1721, a laborer in Aberdeen, a Jacobite in 1745, transported from Liverpool on the Veteran bound for the Leeward Islands on 5 May 1747, liberated and landed on Martinique in June 1747. [NA.SP.36.102][P.3.224]

NESBITT, ROBERT, in Neuilly, Paris, died on 18 May 1839, inventory, 1839, Commissariat of Edinburgh. [NAS]

NEVILL, JOHN, captain of the Greyhound of Brest, a bond, 1680. [NAS.RD4.47.79]

NICHOLL, GEORGE, born 10 September 1721, son of Andrew Nicholl and his wife Margaret Mitchell in Old Machar, Aberdeen, a weaver in Aberdeen, a Jacobite in 1745, transported from Liverpool on the Veteran bound for the Leeward Islands on 5 May 1747, liberated and landed on Martinique in June 1747. [NA.SP.36.102][P.3.226]

NICOLL, JOHN, was admitted as a burgess of Glasgow on 27 September 1627 as he had gone as a soldier to aid in the relief of La Rochelle. [GBR]

NICOLSON, D., in Bordeaux, deeds, 1685. [NAS/RD4.56.530/785]

NISBET, CHARLES, from Edinburgh, graduated MD from Rheims University, 1731. [RCPE] [NAS.NRAS.726.3.57]

NISBET, JAMES, from Edinburgh, a student at Angers University, 1670. [RCPE]

OGILVY of BAMFF, ARCHIBALD, a Captain of *Le Regiment d'Ogilvie*, 1747. [JAHR]

OGILVIE, DAVID, born at Cortachy, Angus, in 1725, son of the Earl of Airlie, educated at Aberdeen University, and at the *Ecole* Militaire in Paris, an officer of the *Regiment Royal Ecossais* in 1744, Jacobite Colonel of Ogilvy's Regiment in 1745, fled via Norway and Sweden to France in 1746, Colonel of *le Regiment d'Ogilvie* 1747. [OR#1][GK#111][JAHR]

OGILVIE, DAVID, a merchant in Coul, Tannadice, Angus, a Jacobite Captain of Ogilvy's Regiment in 1745, fled to Norway in 1746, imprisoned in Bergen, later in France. [OR#2/127][LPR#228]

OGILVIE, JAMES, of Boyne, born 1667, son of Sir Patrick Ogilvie and his wife Anna Grant, a Jacobite who fought at Sheriffmuir in 1715, fled to France in 1716. [JAB#167]

OGILVIE, JAMES, son of James Ogilvie of Boyne and his wife Anna Arnot, a Jacobite Lieutenant Colonel who fled to France in 1716. [JAB#167]

OGILVY, Lady JOANNA, in Montreul, France, died February 1850, inventory, 1850, Comm. Edinburgh. [NAS]

OGILVY, JOHN, of Inchewan, Tannadice, Angus, born 1711, son of John Ogilvy and his wife Mary Keith, Jacobite Paymaster and Captain of Ogilvy's Regiment, fled via Dundee to Norway in 1746, imprisoned in Bergen, later in France, died in 1781. [OR#2/140][LPR#228]

OGILVY, Lady MARGARET, wife of Lord Ogilvy of Airlie, Angus, a Jacobite in 1745, imprisoned in Inverness and in Edinburgh, escaped on 21 November 1746, died in France during 1757. [P.3.240]

OGILVY, THOMAS, of Inverquharity, Kirriemuir, Angus, third son of Sir John Ogilvy and his wife Helen Mercer, Jacobite captain of Ogilvy's Regiment in 1745, fled via Dundee to Bergen and from there to France in 1746, a Captain of *le Regiment d'Ogilvie*, 1747. [JAHR] [OR.3.127/142][LPR#226]

OGILVY, WILLIAM, a Captain of Colonel Hepburn's
Regiment, died in battle at Mons in 1709.
[NAS.GD77.200.1]

OGILVY, WILLIAM, of WHITBURN, a Captain of *Le
Regiment d'Ogilvie,* 1747. [JAHR]

OGILVY of TEST, ..., a Captain of *Le Regiment d'Ogilvie,*
1747. [JAHR]

OGILVY-KENNEDY, WILLIAM, a Captain of *Le Regiment
d'Ogilvie,* 1747. [JAHR]

OGLE, JAMES, a teacher in Guines, France, died on 1 August
1847, inventory, 1848, Commissariat of Edinburgh.
[NAS]

OLIPHANT, WILLIAM, son of Lord Patrick Oliphant and
his wife Mary Crichton, a Jacobite Colonel in 1715, fled
to France in 1716, died in Scotland on 27 December
1728. [JAB#169][SP.VI.559]

ORD, THOMAS, born 1769, Customs Collector and Militia
Colonel, died in Martinique in 1799. [DM.1.539]

ORD, WILLIAM, from Perth, a citizen of Paris and a banker
in Rue de Channerrie, St Eustace, Paris, probate 1684.
[PCC]; a deed of factory, 1683. [NAS.RD4.53.48]

ORR, DUNCAN, born 1706, a laborer in Perthshire, a Jacobite
in 1745, transported from Liverpool on the Veteran
bound for the Leeward Islands on 5 May 1747, liberated
and landed on Martinique in June 1747.
[NA.SP.36.102][P.3.102]

ORR, DUNCAN, born 1733, a weaver in Perthshire, a Jacobite
in 1745, transported from Liverpool on the Veteran
bound for the Leeward Islands on 5 May 1747, liberated
and landed on Martinique in June 1747.
[NA.SP.36.102][P.3.244]

OSBURNE, or CAMBRONNE, MARY, in Nantes, an
inventory, 1872. [NAS.SC70.156/658]

OSWALD, GEORGE, graduated MD from Rheims University in 1723. [NAS.NRAS.726.3.42]

PAE, GEORGE, in Rouen, heir to his aunt Mary, sister of Alexander Pae a joiner in Falkirk, Stirlingshire, 13 November 1844. [NAS.S/H]

PAIP, GILBERT, in Rouen, 1641. [NAS.GD18.2407]

PALLAT, ARNOLD, a merchant in Bordeaux, was admitted as a burgess and guilds-brother of Ayr on 31 July 1686. [ABR]

PALLAT, or PALLOTTE, JEAN, daughter of Peter Pallotte, a merchant in Bordeaux, and spouse of William Baisle, a deed, 1692. [NAS.RD2.75.519]

PALLAT, or PALLOTTE, PETER, a merchant in Bordeaux, 1666, 1669, 1676, 1677, 1683, 1685, 1686, 1687, 1690, deeds. [NAS.RD4.1.403; RD4.41.699; RD2.25.104; RD4.58.263; RD3.22.267; RD3.41.450; RD4.60.690; RD4.56.533; RD4.61.509/942; RD3.74.476]; was admitted as a burgess and guilds-brother of Ayr on 25 July 1664. [ABR]

PALMES, NICOLAS, a mariner on the Happy Amede of Martego (Martinique?), 1714. [NAS.RD4.89.348]

PARK, GEORGE, born on 3 November 1777 in Dunnottar, Kincardineshire, son of William Park and his wife Rebecca Middleton, died in Guadaloupe during 1807. [Fetteresso, Kincardineshire, MI]

PARKER, WILLIAM, 18 Rue Cassini, Paris, died on 5 June 1855, inventory, 1855, Commissariat of Edinburgh. [NAS]

PATERSON, GEORGE, a weaver burgess, second son of Archibald Paterson a weaver burgess, was admitted as a guildsbrother as he had gone to France as a soldier as part of the town's levy, 15 November 1621. [GBR]

PATERSON, ROBERT, born 3 July 1728, son of Abraham Paterson and his wife Elspet Shepherd in Old Machar, Aberdeen, a hosier in Aberdeen, a Jacobite in 1745, transported from Liverpool on the Veteran bound for the Leeward Islands on 5 May 1747, liberated and landed on Martinique in June 1747. [NA.SP.36.102][P.2.248][JAB.2.439]

PATERSON, WILLIAM, graduated MD from Rheims University, 1725. [RCPE]

PATON, DAVID, graduated MD from Rheims University, 1720. [RCPE]

PATTINSON, RICHARD, in Le Havre, heir to his grandfather Jonathan Pattinson a farmer in Kilmarnock, Ayrshire, who died between 1775 and 1783, 23 February 1870. [NAS.Services of Heirs]; an inventory, 1876. [NAS.SC70.178.428]

PATTULLO, GEORGE, graduated MD from Rheims University, 1710; 1714. [RCPE][NAS.NRAS.726.3.27]

PATTULLO, HENRY, a merchant in Dundee, a Jacobite muster master in 1745 who fled via Dundee, Bergen, and Sweden to France in 1746. [LPR#230][GK#118][OR#127]

PAULUS, JOSEPH, a mariner on the Happy Amede of Martego, 1714. [NAS.RD4.89.348]

PEACOCK, JOHN, graduated MD from Rheims University, 1684. [RCPE]

PEDRO, TOBIAS, a merchant in Le Croisic, 1628. [NAS.AC7.1.153]

PEIRCE, ANDREW, a factor at Havre de Grace, 1742. [NAS.GD188.27.4]

PENNICUIK, ALEXANDER, a student at Caen University, 1670. [RCPE]

PETITE, PIERRE, a factor in Rouen, 1742.
[NAS.GD188.27.4]

PETRIE, JAMES, born 1727, a laborer and a Jacobite soldier
of Ogilvy's Regiment in 1745, transported from
Liverpool on the <u>Veteran</u> bound for the Leeward Islands
on 5 May 1747, liberated and landed on Martinique in
June 1747. [P.2.250][OR34][NA.SP.36.102]

PIERRE, NICOLAS, born in Couranvoie, France, a
Lieutenant of the 26th Regiment, captured in Martinique,
a prisoner of war in Valleyfield, Scotland, died there 14
May 1814. [NAS.Adm.list 1821/246;
NA.ADM.103.436/7648, 103.648]

P'FISTRE, PIERRE LOUIS, heir to his grandmother
Margaret Angelique Lamotte or Taverne in Paris, and to
his grand-uncle Pierre Lamote a teacher of dancing, 25
January 1786. [NAS.S/H]

PITCAIRN, ALEXANDER, from Fife, graduated MD from
Rheims University, 1682. [RCPE]

PITCAIRN, ARCHIBALD, was born in Edinburgh in 1652,
and educated at the universities of Edinburgh, Paris and
Rheims between 1670 and 1680, later graduated from
Aberdeen, a physician in Edinburgh, died 1713.
[NAS.NA22807][RCPE]

PITCAIRN, DAVID, from Edinburgh, graduated MD from
Rheims University, 1700. [RCPE]

PLAINE, JAMES, son of Francis Plaine, sometime a
merchant in Paris, died in Savanna, Georgia during
September 1798. Testament confirmed in Edinburgh on
23 February 1807. [NAS.CC8.8]

POPLE, WILLIAM, (partner of Robert Stewart), a factor and
merchant in Bordeaux, 1683, deeds,1678, 1684.
[NAS.AC7.6; RD4.42.481; RD4.52.368; RD4.53.169;
RD2.60.605; RD2.61.279; SE#30]

PORAZ, FRANCOIS, born France 1796, died in 1868, buried in Dundee. [Cortachy, Angus,MI]

PORTERFIELD, WILLIAM, graduated MD from Rheims University, 1717; 1721. [RCPE][NAS.NRAS.726.3.39]

PRESTON, CHARLES, from Edinburgh, graduated MD from Rheims University, 1696, 1704. [RCPE][NAS.NRAS.726.3.14]

PRESTON, JOHN, in Orleans, 1674, letters. [NLS.ms#3864, fos.48-50]

PRIERE, JOSEPH SILAS, born in Le Havre, France, a seaman aboard the L'Amphitrite, captured at sea off Martinique, a prisoner of war in Valleyfield, Scotland, died there 27 May 1814. [NAS.Adm.list 1821/253; NA.ADM.103.434.2197, 103.648]

PRINGLE, JAMES, from Edinburgh, graduated MD from Rheims University, 1733. [RCPE]

PRINGLE, ROBERT, a merchant in Rouen, deeds, 1661, 1678. [NAS.RD4.3.320; RD2.47.413]

PRINGLE, ROBERT, graduated MD from Rheims University, 1741. [RCPE]

PROCTOR, or DYER, Mrs ELIZA, in Brussels, an inventory, 1877. [NAS.SC70.183.761]

PROYE, SIMON, a weaver in Picardy, Edinburgh, son and heir of the late Charles Proye a weaver there, with the consent of his only child Magdalen Proye and her husband John Cartier a tallow chandler in Edinburgh, 1798. [NAS.NG1.66.7]

QUENTIN, JAMES, formerly a professor at the Royal Military School at Louvain, who left France on 20 August 1792, and via London and Edinburgh settled in Perth as a school teacher in 1797. [NAS.B59.24.6.130]

RAINEY, FRANCIS, graduated MD from Rheims University, 1740. [RCPE]

RAITT, GEORGE, from Dundee, graduated MD from Rheims University, 1680; 1708. [RCPE][NAS.GD68.1.277]

RAIT, WILLIAM, from Angus, graduated MD from Rheims University, 1742. [RCPE][NAS.GD68.1.309]

RAMSAY, JOHN, from Forfar, Angus, graduated MD from Rheims University, 1688. [RCPE]

RAMSAY, JOHN, from the Mearns (?),graduated MD from Rheims University, 1696. [RCPE]

RAMSAY, JOHN, from Forfar, Angus, graduated MD from Rheims University, 1688. [RCPE]

RANKINE, HENRY, a factor in La Rochelle, formerly a merchant in Edinburgh, husband of Janet Dunlop, deeds, 1673, 1682. [NAS.RD4.33.107; RD3.53.352]

RANKINE, HENRY, eldest son of Henry Rankine, a merchant in La Rochelle, was admitted as a burgess and guilds-brother of Ayr on 22 June 1671; a factor and merchant in La Rochelle, deeds, 1673, 1679, 1680, 1684. [ABR][NAS.RD4.33.94; RD4.45.34/382; RD2.52.700; RD4.46.515; AC7.6]

RANKINE, WALTER, a factor in Bordeaux, 1680. [NAS.RH15.106.387]

REDPATH, WILLIAM, an archer of the Scots Guards of France, 1560s. [NAS.NRAS.0.143]

REID, GEORGE, born 29 May 1716, son of Walter Reid in Deskford, Banffshire, a laborer in Banff, a Jacobite in 1745, transported from Liverpool on the <u>Veteran</u> bound for the Leeward Islands on 5 May 1747, liberated and landed on Martinique in June 1747. [NA.SP.36.102][JAB.2.440][P.3.266]

REID, JAMES, born 1729, a laborer from Angus, a Jacobite
soldier of Ogilvy's Regiment in 1745, transported from
Liverpool on the Veteran bound for the Leeward Islands
on 5 May 1747, liberated and landed on Martinique in
June 1747. [P.3.266][OR45][NA.T1.328]

REID, MARY CATHERINE, daughter of John Reid, a
Scotsman, was baptised in Notre Dame, Montreal,
October 1715. [Dictionnaire Genealogique des Famille
Canadiennes, Vol.1, fo.574]

REIKILMAN, LIVEN, master of the St Peter of Calais, 1630.
[NAS.AC7.2.291]

RENAUD, ANTHONY, a mariner on the Happy Amede of
Martego, 1714. [NAS.RD4.89.348]

RENALD, PATRICK, graduated MD from Rheims
University, 1724. [RCPE]

RICHARDSON, BARBARA, daughter of James Richardson
of Pitfour, residing in Bagneres de Bigorre, France,
inventory and testament confirmed on 7 September 1840
with the Commissary of Edinburgh. [NAS]

RIDDELL, JAMES, a merchant in Guadaloupe, 1782.
[NAS.CS17.1.1/97]

RIDDELL, JOHN, graduated MD from Rheims University,
1700. [RCPE][NAS.NRAS.726.3.7]

RIDDOCH, JOHN, rector of the Scots College at Douai,
1743-1757. [RSC.I.85/90]

RIGG, JAMES, graduated MD from Rheims University, 1700.
[RCPE]

ROBB, ELIZABETH, born 1712, a knitter in Aberdeen, a
Jacobite in 1745, transported from Liverpool on the
Veteran bound for the Leeward Islands on 5 May 1747,
liberated and landed on Martinique in June 1747.
[NA.SP.36.102][JAB.2.441][P.3.274]

Scots-French Links in Europe and America, 1550-1850

ROBERTSON, ALEXANDER, of Struan, son of Alexander Robertson and his wife Marion Baillie, a Jacobite who fought at Sheriffmuir in 1715, a prisoner who escaped to France in 1716, died in Rannoch, Scotland, on 18 April 1749.]JP#156][MHP#292]

ROBERTSON, ALEXANDER, born 1707, a laborer in Struan, Perthshire, a Jacobite in 1745, transported from Liverpool on the Veteran bound for the Leeward Islands on 5 May 1747, liberated and landed on Martinique in June 1747. [NA.SP.36.102][P.3.276]

ROBERTSON, DONALD, a Captain of *Le Regiment d'Ogilvie*, 1759. [JAHR]

ROBERTSON, JAMES, from Edinburgh, graduated MD from Rheims University, 1686. [RCPE]

ROBERTSON, JOHN, born 1728, a laborer in Inverness, a Jacobite in 1745, transported from Liverpool on the Veteran bound for the Leeward Islands on 5 May 1747, liberated and landed on Martinique in June 1747. [NA.SP.36.102][P.3.278]

ROBERTSON, PHILADELPHIA JANE, in Pau, France, an inventory, 1871. [NAS.SC70.152.283]

ROBERTSON, WILLIAM, a merchant in Bordeaux, a bond. 1673. [NAS.RD4.34.113]

ROBERTSON, WILLIAM, born 1727, a weaver in Spynie, Morayshire, a Jacobite in 1745, transported from Liverpool on the Veteran bound for the Leeward Islands on 5 May 1747, liberated and landed on Martinique in June 1747. [NA.SP.36.102][P.3.280]

ROBERTSON, WILLIAM, born 1730, a laborer in Perth, a Jacobite in 1745, transported from Liverpool on the Veteran bound for the Leeward Islands on 5 May 1747, liberated and landed on Martinique in June 1747. [NA.SP.36.102][P.3.280]

ROBERTSON of BLAIRFETTY, ..., a Captain of *le Regiment d'Albanie*, 1748. [JAHR]

ROLLAND, GEORGE, graduated MD from Rheims University, 1787. [RCPE]

ROSE, ALEXANDER, from Aberdeen, graduated MD from Rheims University, 1727. [RCPE]

ROSS, CATHERINE ROSE, daughter of Hugh Rose Ross of Cromarty, married Thomas Knox Holmes in Brussels on 17 July 1848. [AJ#5246][EEC#21686]

ROSS, DANIEL, born 1707, a servant in Ross-shire, a Jacobite in 1745, transported from Liverpool on the Veteran bound for the Leeward Islands on 5 May 1747, liberated and landed on Martinique in June 1747. [NA.SP.36.102][P.3.286]

ROSS, DAVID, graduated MD from Rheims University, 1726. [RCPE]

ROSS, JAMES, born 1727, a carpenter in Edinburgh, a Jacobite in 1745, transported from Liverpool on the Veteran bound for the Leeward Islands on 5 May 1747, liberated and landed on Martinique in June 1747. [NA.SP.36.102][P.3.288]

ROSS, WILLIAM, born 1711, a sailor in Aberdeenshire, a Jacobite in 1745, transported from Liverpool on the Veteran bound for the Leeward Islands on 5 May 1747, liberated and landed on Martinique in June 1747. [NA.SP.36.102][P.3.290]

RUSSEL, ALEXANDER, born 1855, only son of William Russel of Kininmonth, Aberdeenshire, died in Cannes on 23 December 1875. [AJ#6681]

RUSSEL, THOMAS, born 1772, son of Thomas Russel of Rathen and his wife Anna Innes, died in Martinique during July 1794. [Banff MI]

RUSSELL, WILLIAM, a merchant in Wigtown trading with Rouen and Nantes, 1700-1704. [NAS.CS96.1145]

RUTHERFORD, Lord ANDREW, a Lieutenant General under the King of France, 1661. [RGS.XI.32]

RUTHERFORD, JOHN, graduated MD from Rheims University, 1719. [RCPE]

RUTHERFORD, JOHN, graduated MD from Rheims University in 1724. [NAS.NRAS.724.3.45]

RUTHERFORD, JOHN, graduated MD from Rheims University, 1729. [RCPE]

RUTHERFORD, THOMAS, from Jedburgh, graduated MD from Rheims University, 1736. [RCPE]

RUTHERFORD, WILLIAM, from Jedburgh, graduated MD from Rheims University, 1681. [RCPE]

RUTHVEN, JOHN, a Captain of the Earl of Dunfermline's Regiment in France, 1676. [NAS.RD4.39.199]

ST CLAIR, JAMES, in St Pierre, Martinique, letters, 1796. [NAS.GD503.151; NRAS.16/13]

SAMPSON, R., a wine merchant in Bordeaux, 1720s. [NAS.NRAS.2362/316]

SAMPSON and SANDILANDS, factors in Bordeaux, around 1718. [NAS.GD377.399]

SAMUEL, GEORGE, born 1729, a bookbinder in Edinburgh, a Jacobite in 1745, transported from Liverpool on the Veteran bound for the Leeward Islands on 5 May 1747, liberated and landed on Martinique in June 1747. [NA.SP.36.102][P.3.298]

SANDERSON, GLAS, of Bonskeid, Perthshire, died in Montpellier, France, on 3 October 1835. [Perth, Greyfriars, MI]

SANDILANDS, ALEXANDER, graduated MD from Rheims University, 1704. [RCPE]

SANDILANDS, GEORGE, possibly from Aberdeen, a merchant in Bordeaux, 1723. [NAS.NRAS.2847/1/46]

SANDILANDS, GEORGE, in Bordeaux, was admitted as a burgess of St Andrews on 6 April 1774. [SABR]

SANDILANDS, JACOB, a merchant in Bordeaux, eldest son and heir of George Sandilands of Cotton, Aberdeenshire, a merchant in Bordeaux, 29 July 1755, genealogy, 1 June 1773. [NAS.Lyon Office. GI.41/208]

SAUNDERS, JANE MEGGET, youngest daughter of James Saunders, a physician in Edinburgh, married Professor Charles Frederick Gerhardt in the Protestant Temple. Montpellier, on 22 May 1844. [W.V.469]

SCHALCHER, EULAI, born during 1815 in Lorraine, a dress-maker residing in Edinburgh by 1851. [Census]

SCOTT, ALEXANDER, graduated MD from Rheims University, 1713; 1725. [RCPE][NAS.NRAS.726.3.49]

SCOTT, GEORGE, of Hedderwick, Forfar,Angus, died in Paris on 19 August 1854. [W.XV.1576]

SCOTT, JOHN, born 1730, a herd in Atholl, Perthshire, a Jacobite in 1745, transported from Liverpool on the Veteran bound for the Leeward Islands on 5 May 1747, liberated and landed on Martinique in June 1747. [NA.SP.36.102][MR209]

SCOTT, LUCY, in Tarbes, France, an inventory, 1873. [NAS.SC70.161.343]

SCOTT, MARGARET, late of Ancrum, died in Caen on 14 May 1849, inventory, 1864, Commissariat of Edinburgh. [NAS]

SCOTT, ROBERT, in Paris, 1700. [NAS.RD4.86.369]

SCOTT, WILLIAM, master of the Catherine of Bordeaux, a vendition, 1669. [NAS.RD2.25.196]

SCOTT, Mrs, widow of Michael Scott in Grenada, married Count De La Basecque, in Artois, France, in November 1792. [GM.84.697]

SCOULAR, JAMES, brother of John Scoular, a merchant and factor in Rouen, deeds, 1685, 1687, 1689. [NAS.RD4.57.440; RD2.68.904; RD4.64.17]

SCOULAR, JOHN, a merchant residing in France, was admitted as a burgess and guildsbrother of Glasgow on 12 July 1669, by right of being the eldest son of William Scoular a merchant burgess and guildsbrother of Glasgow. [GBR] a merchant and factor in Rouen, a deed, 1672; dead by 1686. [NAS.AC7.7; RD4.31.425; RD4.45.166; RD2.74.963; RD4.47.73; RD4.64.17]

SEATON, GEORGE, graduated MD from Rheims University, 1719. [RCPE]

SEC, ALEXANDRE, born in Cassel during 1761, a seaman aboard the Vigilant captured in the West Indies, a prisoner of war in Greenlaw, Scotland, died there 16 September 1805. [NA.ADM103/155/171; 103/624]

SELLAR, THOMAS, born in Mowick, Shetland, on 12 January 1820, a merchant in New York from 1840 to 1846, died in Cannes on 22 October 1885. [ANY.2.239]

SEMPILL, JOHN, a Captain of Grenadiers in *Le Regiment d'Ogilvie*, 1747. [JAHR]

SEMPILL, ROBERT, born 1672 son of Archibald Sempill, a French Army officer who was sent from Calais, France to Aberdeen, Scotland to aid the Jacobites in 1715, died in Paris during 1737. [JAB#179][JP#164][NA.SP54.11.181]

SENNE, PIERRE JACQUES, a seaman aboard the privateer La Liberte captured off Jamaica, a prisoner of war in

Greenlaw, Scotland, died there 10 July 1808.
[NA.ADM.103.155/206, 103.624, 103.648]

SETON, GEORGE, a Captain of the Earl of Dunfermline's
Regiment in France, 1676. [NAS.RD4.39.199]

SEYTOUN, JOHN, a Captain of the King of France's Guards,
1627. [NAS.GD7.2.33]

SHARP, WILLIAM, born 1729, a laborer in Aberdeen, a
Jacobite in 1745, transported from Liverpool on the
Veteran bound for the Leeward Islands on 5 May 1747,
liberated and landed on Martinique in June 1747.
[NA.SP.36.102][JAB.2.442][P.3.308]

SHAW, ALEXANDER, a prisoner in Edinburgh Tolbooth
who was released to go to France as a soldier on 4
February 1676. [RPCS.3/IV.668]

SHAW, CHARLES, graduated MD from Rheims University,
1734. [RCPE]

SHAW, JAMES, a prisoner in Edinburgh Tolbooth who was
released to go to France as a soldier on 4 February 1676.
[RPCS.3/IV.668]

SHAW, JOHN, graduated MD from Rheims University, 1726.
[RCPE]

SHAW, ROBERT, a prisoner in Edinburgh Tolbooth who was
released to go to France as a soldier on 4 February 1676.
[RPCS.3/IV.668]

SIBBALD, Sir ROBERT, a student at Angers University,
1662. [RCPE]

SIBELLET, JOHN, a servant to Patrick La Laine a factor in
Bordeaux, was admitted as a burgess of Ayr on 25 June
1687. [ABR]

SINCLAIR, ANDREW, a student at Angers University, 1720.
[RCPE]

SINCLAIR, JOHN, graduated MD from Rheims University, 1703. [RCPE]

SINCLAIR, PATRICK, graduated MD from Rheims University, 1703. [RCPE]

SINCLAIR, WILLIAM, from Caithness, graduated MD from Rheims University, 1738. [RCPE]

SKINNER, DAVID, a merchant in Bordeaux, son of Robert Skinner a land-waiter in the Port of Aberdeen, 1766. [NAS.RS35.21.344]

SKINNER, HERCULES, a merchant in Montrose, Angus, formerly a merchant in Bordeaux, 1762. [NAS.RS35.XX.5]

SKINNER, JOHN, a merchant in Bordeaux, son of David Skinner of Cononsyth, Angus, 1702. [NAS.RS35.20.5]

SMAILHOLM, JOHN, graduated MD from Rheims University, 1693. [RCPE]

SMITH, DANIEL, a merchant in Bordeaux, eldest son of Donald Smith a bailie of Ayr, 1650; a bond, 10 October 1661. [NAS.GD1.521.15; RD2.2.773]

SMITH, or Du REGE, ELIZABETH, in France, heir to her grand-uncle Alexander Coutts of Redfield, 1771. [NAS.S/H]

SMITH, HUGH, of Boulogne, France, married Elizabeth Seton of Touch, in Linlithgow, West Lothian, 21 September 1745. [DUAS: BrMS3/Dc/12]

SMITH, JAMES, from Aberdeen, graduated MD from Rheims University, 1736. [RCPE]

SMITH, JAMES, a merchant in Bordeaux, was admitted as a burgess of St Andrews, Fife, on 4 April 1740. [SAU; Burgh Court Book]

SMITH, JOHN, born 1726, a goldsmith in Aberdeen, a
Jacobite in 1745, transported from Liverpool on the
Veteran bound for the Leeward Islands on 5 May 1747,
liberated and landed on Martinique in June 1747.
[NA.SP.36.102][p.3.322][JAB.2.443]

SMITH, THOMAS STEWART, of Glassingall, Perthshire,
died in Avignon on 31 December 1869. [Holy Rude MI,
Stirling]

SOMERVILLE, PETER, born in 1732, a shoemaker, a
Jacobite drummer of Ogilvy's Regiment in 1745,
transported from Liverpool on the Veteran bound for the
Leeward Islands on 5 May 1747, liberated and landed on
Martinique in June 1747. [P.2.236][NA.SP.36.102]

SPEARS, CATHERINE, born 1809, daughter of Robert
Spears of Kininmont and his wife Margaret Millie, died
in Paris on 21 May 1827. [Cupar, Fife, gravestone]

SPENCE, ISABELLA, born 1820, daughter of John Spence
and his wife Ann Ritchie, died in Brussels 21 January
1841. [Errol MI]

SPENCE, THOMAS, from Edinburgh, graduated MD from
Rheims University, 1683. [RCPE]

SPITTAL, JOHN, a millwright in Prince Edward Island, died
in Rouen on 8 March 1861, inventory, 1862,
Commissariat of Edinburgh. [NAS]

SPROT, ALEXANDER, the younger of Garnkirk, died in Pau
on 16 February 1854. [W.XV.1519]

STEDMAN, JOHN, from Lothian, graduated MD from
Rheims University, 1740. [RCPE]

STEEDMAN, JOHN, graduated MD from Rheims University
in 1764. [NAS.NRAS.726.3.102]

STEELE, or HILL, Mrs J. CLARKE, in Brussels, an
inventory, 1876. [NAS.SC70.179.542]

STENTHAL, FRANCIS ANTON, died in Pau on 9 December 1864, inventory, 1865, Commissariat of Edinburgh. [NAS]

STERLING, JAMES, a Captain of Le Regiment d'Albanie, 1748. [JAHR]

STERLING, PHILIP, sent by the King of France on the La Marie, Captain Tapic to Louisiana on 28 May 1719. [NWI.I.490]

STERLING, ..., a Captain of Le Regiment Royal Ecossais, 1747. [JAHR]

STEVENSON, ALEXANDER, a banker in Paris, 1714. [NAS.RD2.85.76]

STEVENSON, GEORGE, from Edinburgh, graduated MD from Rheims University, 1749. [RCPE]

STEVENSON, JAMES, graduated MD from Rheims University, 1705, son of the late William Stevenson MD. [RCPE] [NAS.NRAS.726.3.17]

STEWART, ANTONY, born 1739, a student at Douai, 1751. [RSC.I.88]

STEWART, JAMES, of Cardonell, a former Captain of the Scots Guards of France, died on 5 January 1584. [Paisley Abbey MI]

STEWART, JAMES, graduated MD from Rheims University in 1721. [NAS.NRAS.726.3.40]

STEWART, JOHN, from Lothian, graduated MD from Rheims University, 1740; 1744. [RCPE][NAS.NRAS.726.3.70]

STEWART, JOHN, born 1729, a laborer in Aberdeen, a Jacobite in 1745, transported from Liverpool on the Veteran bound for the Leeward Islands on 5 May 1747, liberated and landed on Martinique in June 1747. [NA.SP.36.102][JAB.2.443][P.3.346]

STEWART, JOHN, born 1730, a laborer in Perthshire, a
Jacobite in 1745, transported from Liverpool on the
Veteran bound for the Leeward Islands on 5 May 1747,
liberated and landed on Martinique in June 1747.
[NA.SP.36.102]

STEWART, JOHN, the younger of Allanbank, married Agnes,
daughter of Charles Smith of Boulogne, France, at Murray's
Hall near Stirling, 9 October 1750. [DUAS: BrMS3/Dc/12]

STEWART, ROBERT, a merchant in Bordeaux, son of
Provost James Stewart of Edinburgh, deeds, 1672, 1673,
1674, 1677, 1678, 1683, 1687. [NAS.RD2.32.59/300;
RD3.34.44; RD3.36.287; RD4.40.788; RD2.43.511;
RH15.106.163.5; RD4.42.157/481; RD4.52.368;
RD4.53.170/258; RD4.61.322]; a factor in Bordeaux,
was admitted as a burgess and guilds-brother of Ayr on 1
October 1673; a factor in Rouen then in Edinburgh,
1684. [ABR][NAS.AC7/6][SE#30]

STEWART, ROBERT, Lieutenant of the 61st Regiment, son
of James Stewart of Urrard, Perthshire, died in
Martinique on 28 June 1795. [CM#11597]

STEWART, WILLIAM, the younger of Galston, an archer of
the Scots Guards of France, 1560s. [NAS.NRAS.0.143]

STEWART, WILLIAM, from Islay, Argyll, was admitted as a
burgess of Glasgow on 27 September 1627 as he had
gone as a soldier to aid in the relief of La Rochelle.
[GBR]

STEWART, WILLIAM, from Jamaica, married Maria Odelia
van Hoogmert, daughter of Gerevid van Hoogmert a
merchant in La Rochelle, in Edinburgh on 3 January
1780. [Edinburgh Marriage Register]

STEWART, ..., Lieutenant of the Royal Engineers, died in St
Domingo, 1796. [NAS.GD188.28.6]

STIRLING, WALTER, graduated MD from Rheims
University, 1737. [RCPE]

STORY, ..., a Lieutenant of Grenadiers in *Le Regiment d'Ogilvy*, 1747-1757. [JAHR]

STRACHAN, ALEXANDER, settled in France around 1648. [SE#27]

STRACHAN, ALEXANDER, from Aberdeen, graduated MD from Rheims University, 1720. [RCPE]

STRACHAN, KENNETH FRANCIS, educated at the Scots College at Douai 1700, later rector of the Scots College in Madrid, 1725. [RSC.I.65/203[

STRACHAN, ROBERT, born 1737, son of Alexander Strachan and Joanna Bremner, educated at Douai in 1758. [RSC.I.91]

STRAITON, DANIEL, a factor at St Martin's, was admitted as a burgess and guilds-brother of Ayr on 13 August 1713, [ABR]; a merchant in St Martin's, France, testament confirmed in Edinburgh on 25 May 1720. [NAS]

STRANG, JOHN, a merchant and factor in Bordeaux, 1688, in London by 1692, deeds. [NAS.RD3.69.456; RD4.70.156]

STRONG, JOHN, graduated MD from Rheims University, 1736. [RCPE]

STUART, DONALD, an officer of *Le Regiment Royal Ecossais*, 1744. [JAHR]

STUART, JAMES, an archer of the Scots Guards of France, 1560s. [NAS.NRAS.0.143]

STUART, JAMES, graduated MD from Rheims University, 1720. [RCPE]

STUART, JAMES, a Captain of Grenadiers in *Le Regiment d'Ogilvie*, 1750. [JAHR]

STUART, JOHN, a Lieutenant of Grenadiers in *Le Regiment d'Ogilvy*, 1757. [JAHR]

STUART, JOSEPH, a Captain of *Le Regiment Royal Ecossais*, 1745-1759. [JAHR]

STUART, PATRICK, graduated MD from Rheims University, 1707. [RCPE]

STUART, PETER, a Captain of *Le Regiment d'Ogilvie*, 1747. [JAHR]

STUART, THOMAS, an archer of the Scots Guards of France, 1560s. [NAS.NRAS.0.143]

STUART, WILLIAM, a Captain of *Le Regiment d'Ogilvie*, 1763. [JAHR]

STUART, WILLIAM, aged 53, with his wife aged 37, and children George aged 18, Michael aged 12, Sally aged 10, David aged 8, Rachel aged 6, and Mary aged 2, settled in Louisiana in 1797. [NWI.II.230]

SURENNE, DANIEL FERDINAND, a teacher of Drawing in Edinburgh, died 8 May 1861, inventory, 1859, Comm. Edinburgh. [NAS]

SURENNE, GABRIEL, a teacher of French in Edinburgh, died 12 September 1858, inventory, 1859, Comm. Edinburgh. [NAS]

SUTHERLAND, ADAM, born 1691, a laborer in Sutherland, a Jacobite in 1745, transported from Liverpool on the Veteran bound for the Leeward Islands on 5 May 1747, liberated and landed on Martinique in June 1747. [NA.SP.36.102][P.3.358]

SUTHERLAND, ALEXANDER, from Morayshire, graduated MD from Rheims University, 1740. [RCPE]

SYMMER, JOHN, graduated MD from Rheims University, 1728. [RCPE]

TAWSE, CHRISTINA, born 1821, daughter of George Tawse (1794-1872) and his wife Catherine (1800-1881), died in Lille, France, on 6 August 1866. [Dundee, Eastern Necropolis, gravestone]

THELMAR, FRANCOIS, a doctor on the Happy Amede of Martego, 1714. [NAS.RD4.89.348]

THOM, ROBERT, born in 1731, a laborer in Forfar, Angus, a Jacobite soldier of Ogilvy's Regiment in 1745, transported from Liverpool on the Veteran bound for the Leeward Islands on 5 May 1747, liberated and landed on Martinique in June 1747. [P.2.370][OR52][NA.SP.36.102]

THOMSON, Lieutenant Colonel DAVID, of Mannoire, France, bonds, 1674, 1676. [NAS.RD4.36.233; RD4.40.84, etc]

THOMPSON, JAMES, born 1726, a gardener in Fingask, Kinnaird, Perthshire, a Jacobite in 1745, transported from Liverpool on the Veteran bound for the Leeward Islands on 5 May 1747, liberated and landed on Martinique in June 1747. [NA.SP.36.102][P.3.372]

THOMPSON, JOHN, born 18 June 1730 in Rathven, Banffshire, son of William Thompson and his wife Margaret Innes, a Jacobite in 1745, transported from Liverpool on the Veteran bound for the Leeward Islands on 5 May 1747, liberated and landed on Martinique in June 1747. [NA.SP.36.102][JAB.2.446][P.3.372]

THOMSON, JOHN, a workman in Wardend, Lintrathen, Angus, a Jacobite soldier of Ogilvy's regiment in 1745, fled via Dundee to Norway and then to France in 1746. [OR.52/166]

THOMSON, ROBERT, graduated MD from Rheims University in 1716. [NAS.NRAS.726.3.32]

THOMSON, SUSANNAH, daughter of the late Thomas Thomson a merchant in Leith, died in France on 25

December 1840, inventory, 1842, Comm. Edinburgh.
[NAS]

THOMSON, THOMAS, Colonel of the Scots Guards of
France, 1560s. [NAS.NRAS.0.143]

THOMSON, THOMAS, in Rouen, 1640s. [NAS.GD18.2414]

THOMSON, WILLIAM, born 1707, a workman from Little
Kenny, Lintrathen, Angus, a Jacobite soldier of Ogilvy's
Regiment in 1745, transported from Liverpool on the
Veteran bound for the Leeward Islands on 5 May 1747,
liberated and landed on Martinique in June 1747.
[P.3.372][OR52][NA.SP.36.102]

TOD, WILLIAM, a merchant tailor in Rouen, 1635-1639,
later in Fraserburgh, Aberdeenshire, 1652.
[NAS.GD18.2371][RGS.X.46]

TOD, WILLIAM, a merchant in Rouen, a deed, 1672.
[NAS.RD2.32.462]

TOURS, Colonel JOHN, brother of Major Robert Tours, of
the Scots Guards in French Service, 1666.
[NAS.RD2.15.556]

TOWER, ALEXANDER, born 1801, died in Paris on 3
August 1866, buried in Montmartre. [Edinburgh, St
Cuthbert's, MI]

TROOP, JOHN, born 1727, a gardener in Stirling, a Jacobite
in 1745, transported from Liverpool on the Veteran
bound for the Leeward Islands on 5 May 1747, liberated
and landed on Martinique in June 1747.
[NA.SP.36.102][P.3.378]

TUREIN, ..., servant of M. de Cangee, was admitted as a
burgess and guilds-brother of Ayr on 8 November 1658.
[ABR]

TURNER, JOHN, a citizen of Paris, a deed of factory,
1670,1688, [NAS.RD4.27.35; RD3.67.516], and his wife

Marjory Menzies, testament confirmed in Edinburgh on 21 June 1716. [NAS]

TWEEDIE, JAMES, a cordiner in Paris, 1640s. [NAS.GD18.2371]

TWEEDIE, THOMAS, a prisoner in Edinburgh Tolbooth who was released to go to France as a soldier on 4 February 1676. [RPCS.3/IV.668]

TYRIE, ANDREW, one of the 25 archers of the King's Guard at Fontainbleau, testament confirmed in Edinburgh on 17 June 1608. [NAS]

URQUHART, ADAM, an officer of *Le Regiment Royal Ecossais*, 1744. [JAHR]

URQUHART, CHARLES, born 1688, son of Thomas Urquhart and Anna Adamson, educated at the Scots College in Douai, 1695. [RSC.I.55]

URQUHART, JAMES, born 1729, a laborer in Aberdeenshire, a Jacobite in 1745, transported from Liverpool on the <u>Veteran</u> bound for the Leeward Islands on 5 May 1747, liberated and landed on Martinique in June 1747. [NA.SP.36.102][P.3.382][JAB.2.446]

URQUHART, LUDOVICK, born 1680, educated at the Scots College in Douai, 1695. [RSC.I.63]

VAN DER STRAETEN, PHILIP, a merchant in Bordeaux and in Bruges, bonds, 1673. [NAS.RD2.34.794/785; RD4.33.558/648; RD4.34.387]

WADE, J., in Martinique, 1799. [SA#260]

WALKINSHAW, ROBERT, a writer from Glasgow, son of James Walkinshaw a merchant in Paisley, died in Montauban on 28 April 1821. [S#5.257]

WALLACE, JAMES, a factor in a French port, a deed, 1715. [NAS.RD4.117.883]

WALLACE, JOHN, born in Arbroath during 1654, educated at the Scots College in Paris 1687, Bishop of Edinburgh, 1720, died in Edinburgh, 1733. [SCP.211]

WARREN, ROBERT, born 1727, a weaver in Aberdeenshire or Banffshire, a Jacobite in 1745, transported from Liverpool on the Veteran bound for the Leeward Islands on 5 May 1747, liberated and landed on Martinique in June 1747. [NA.SP.36.102][P.3.390][JAB.2.446]

WEIR, THOMAS, of Bogangreen, died 6 April 1847 in Paris, inventory, 1849, Comm. Edinburgh. [NAS]

WEMYSS,......, Colonel of *Le Regiment Royal Ecossais*, 1757- 1762. [JAHR]

WHITE, THOMAS CORKER, Professor of English Literature and Moral Philosophy at the University of Macon, France, died 6 April 1860, inventory 1860, Comm. Edinburgh. [NAS]

WHITELAW, ROBERT, a student at Montpellier University, 1611. [RCPE]

WHYTE, ROBERT, graduated MD from Rheims University, 1737. [NAS.NRAS.726.3.62]

WHYTE, THOMAS, a merchant in Bordeaux, was admitted as a burgess and guilds-brother of Ayr on 31 September 1700; a deed, 1705. [ABR][NAS.RD3.105.228]

WIGHTON, DAVID, born 1814, son of Robert Wighton, (1764-1843), a farmer near Dundee, and his wife Janet Spark, (1780-1849), died in Port au Prince, St Domingo, 6 January 1840. [Dundee, Constitution Road, gravestone]

WILLIAMSON, THOMAS, son of William Williamson of Cromarty, who went to France in 1410 in the retinue of Lady Margaret, daughter of King James I, who married Louis, Dauphin of France, [NAS.Lyon Office.GI.36, 15/199]

WILLIAMSON, THOMAS, of the Kingdom of France, descended from Thomas Williamson, an archer of the Scots Company of King Francis' Life Guards, who passed into France in 1495, 19 April 1774. [NAS.Lyon Office.GI.219]

WILLIAMSON, WILLIAM, a cooper in Dundee, a Jacobite soldier of Ogilvy's Regiment in 1745, transported from Liverpool on the Veteran bound for the Leeward Islands on 5 May 1747, liberated and landed on Martinique in June 1747. [P.3.402][OR54][NA.SP.36.102]

WILSON, JOHN, in Tours, nephew of William Wilson, an ironmaster in Kinneil, West Lothian, who died on 24 September 1862. [NAS.SH.1880]

WISHART, or DONALDSON, JOHN, born 1633, son of William Wishart and Joanna Cunningham, a student at the Scots College at Douai, 1681. [RSC.I.55]

WOOD, JOHN, a Gentleman at Arms in Gordon's Company in the service of Louis XIII, 1625. [NAS.RH1.2.447]

WOOD, PATRICK, in Paris, a deed, 1684. [NAS.RD4.54.15]

ZORILLA, PEDRO GONZALEZ, in Bayonne, died 11 Sep.1855, inventory, 1857, Comm. Edinburgh. [NAS]

ZWINGLE, M. A., born in France during 1786, a professor of dancing in Edinburgh by 1851. [Census]

SOME SHIPPING LINKS

AMITY OF AYR, master William Reid, arrived at Port South Potomac, Virginia, on 20 November 1752 via France. [VaGaz#101]

ANN, master John Francis, arrived in Greenock from Guadaloupe, 24 October 1763; master Robert Davidson, from Greenock to Guadaloupe in March 1764; arrived in Greenock on 26 January 1765 from Guadaloupe. [NAS.E504.15.12]

BETSY, master John Gillies, from Glasgow via Dunkirk, France, bound for Virginia, arrived in the James River on 2 February 1767. [VaGaz: 30.5.1766]

BOGLE, master Andrew Sym, arrived in the Upper District of the James River, Virginia, on 21 August 1745 from Glasgow via France. [VaGaz#480]

BRILLIANT, master Robert Bennet, arrived in the Upper District of the James River, Virginia, on 16 June 1769 from Glasgow via Bordeaux, France. [VaGaz#946]

BROTHERS OF AYR, master John Macklewraith, arrived at the Port of South Potomac, Virginia, on 7 August 1752 via Dieppe, France. [VaGaz#94]

BRUNSWICK, master Robert Steel, arrived in the James River, Virginia, during June 1767 from Glasgow via Bordeaux, France. [VaGaz#837]

CHARLOTTE OF CALAIS, a French privateer, master Henry Malcolm, a Scot, 1675. [NAS.AC7.4]

CLYDE RIVER, master Adam McLeish, arrived in Greenock on 9 October 1761 from Guadaloupe; from Greenock to Guadaloupe in January 1762; from Greenock to Guadaloupe in December 1762. [NAS.E504.15.10/11]

COCHRANE OF GLASGOW, master William Semple, arrived at Port Rappahannock, Virginia, on 7 July 1752 from Glasgow via Bordeaux, France. [VaGaz#84]

CONCORD OF AYR, master Hugh Moodie, arrived at the Port of South Potomac, Virginia, on 2 October 1752 via France. [VaGaz#94]

DIANA, master Archibald Williamson, from Greenock to Guadaloupe in April 1761; from Greenock to Guadaloupe, in November 1761. [NAS.E504.15.10]

DISPATCH OF GREENOCK, from Greenock to Martinique, in September 1796. [NAS.E504.15.73]

GLASGOW, master Alexander Smith, from Greenock to Martinique in May 1765. [NAS.E504.15.11]

HOPE OF KIRKCALDY, from Dieppe to Brazil, 1630. [NAS.AC7.2.326]

HOUSTON, master James Orr, from Greenock to Martinique in September 1762. [NAS.E504.15.11]

JEANY, master James Orr, arrived in Greenock from Guadaloupe, 1760. [NAS.E504.15.10]

JENNY, master Robert Pooley, from Greenock to Guadaloupe in December 1761. [NAS.E504.15.10]

JOHNSTON, master Andrew Troop, arrived in the James River, Virginia, during April 1767 from Glasgow via Havre de Grace, France. [VaGaz#831]

MALLY, master George Buchanan, from Greenock to Guadaloupe in September 1760. [NAS.E504.15.9]

MALLY, master Robert Bennett, arrived in the James River, Virginia, on 14 August 1767 from Glasgow via Cette, France. [VaGaz#848]

MARS, master James Weir, from Port Glasgow *with passengers* to St Kitts and Guadaloupe on 6 October

1750; master James Weir, from Greenock to Guadaloupe in March 1761. [Aberdeen Journal#665] [NAS.E504.15.10]

MARTHA, master John Robertson, arrived in the Upper District of the James River, Virginia, on 2 May 1766 via Dunkirk, France. [VaGaz#782]

MARTINE OF BAYONNE, master Michael Hause, from Greenland, stranded on Caithness 1676. [NAS.AC7.4]

MATILDA, master Malcolm Dugald, from the Clyde to Martinique in 1796. [NAS.AC7.73]

MENNY, master Alexander Thomson, from Greenock to Guadaloupe in May 1762. [NAS.E504.15.11]

NELLY OF GLASGOW, master Archibald Galbreath, arrived at Port Rappahannock, Virginia, on 4 May 1752 from Glasgow via Havre de Grace, France. [VaGaz#84]

NELLY, master James Corbet, arrived in Greenock from Guadaloupe on 3 July 1761. [NAS.E504.15.10]

PATRIOT PITT, master John Cousins, arrived in Greenock from Martinique in May 1763. [NAS.E504.15.11; CS95.506]

PEGGY, master Thomas Ramsay, arrived in the Upper District of the James River, Virginia, on 14 April 1769 from Glasgow via Cette, France. [VaGaz#935]

ST ANDREW OF DUMFRIES, master Andrew Kennedy, arrived at the Port of South Potomac, Virginia, on 17 August 1752 via France. [VaGaz#94]

THISTLE, master Robert Baird, from Greenock to Martinique in January 1763. [NAS.E504.15.11]

WALTER, Captain Hunter, arrived in the James River, Virginia, in January 1773 from Glasgow via France. [VaGaz#1120]